. . . Courage is a man who keeps on — coming on! Yes, you can slow a man like that, but you can't stop him. The man who keeps coming on — is either going to get there himself — or he is going to make it possible for a later man to get there.

L. H. McNelly, *Captain, Texas Rangers*

RANGERS OF TEXAS

Foreword by
Colonel Wilson E. Speir

Introduction by
Rupert N. Richardson

Original Paintings by
David Sanders

Roger N. Conger

James M. Day

Joe B. Frantz

Ben Procter

Billy Mac Jones

Harold B. Simpson

Dorman H. Winfrey

TEXIAN PRESS   1969   **WACO, TEXAS**

Copyright 1969

by

Texian Press

Printed in the United States of America, all rights reserved. No part of this book may be used or reproduced in any manner whatsoever without written permission, except in the case of brief quotations embodied in critical articles and reviews.

Library of Congress Catalog Card Number

75 - 98305

FIRST EDITION

Published

by

P. O. Box 1684
Waco, Texas

Bound by
LIBRARY BINDING CO.
Waco, Texas

This book is dedicated to the present Texas Rangers. Their courage and devotion to duty have maintained the honor and history of this unique group. They continue to perform in the highest traditions of the Ranger service.

Foreword

By

COLONEL WILSON E. SPEIR, *Director*
Department of Public Safety and
Chief, Texas Rangers

The history of the Texas Rangers is, in a sense, the history of Texas itself. Although there is some uncertainty about the initial organization of this force of officers, it appears that Rangers actually were first employed by Stephen F. Austin in 1823.

Two years earlier, Austin was granted permission by the Mexican government to bring 300 families of colonists to the territory of Texas, and by 1823 it was apparent that some kind of protective body was needed to insure their safety from marauding Indians.

Austin then conceived the idea of the Rangers and employed ten men from a group of volunteers. They were ordered to range over wide areas between designated rivers and to scout the movements of the Indians. From these ranging activities, the Rangers derived their name.

On the eve of the Texas War of Independence from Mexico in October, 1835, the General Assembly, impressed by the success of the Rangers, and recognizing the need for an organization to protect the frontier, took the necessary action to organize the Texas Ranger Force.

During the period of the Texas Revolution, they were busy protecting the settlers from the Indians. Following Texas' independence from Mexico in 1836 the Rangers, who had been placed under the commander-in-chief of the military forces of Texas, were instrumental in curbing the activities of cattle thieves and other outlaws, as well as carrying out their initial protective duty.

The rugged fighting prowess of the Texas Rangers, already almost legendary, received another boost of recognition at the time Texas joined the Union in 1845. The national government thought that it could do without the Rangers, and sent regular West Point-trained U. S. troops to police the Texas borders. After a few brief encounters with Indians, the War Department "invited" the Rangers to serve along with the regulars.

One of General Zachary Taylor's staff members once said of the Rangers: "They are not only the eyes and ears of General Taylor's army, but its right and left arms as well."

During the period from 1874 to 1880 when the so-called "Frontier Battalion" was under the command of Major John B. Jones, the Rangers fought on three fronts. Bandits and cattle rustlers were rampant in the Rio Grande Valley, Indians were still ravaging the western border, and white outlaws—a growing threat—were robbing and looting within the settlements.

In August of 1876, General William Steele reported that lawlessness by white people was becoming more of a problem than Indian raids. The Rangers were forced to learn new techniques—not those of soldier-scout and Indian fighter, but rather those of the detective and police officer. They met the challenge with their unique brand of determination and their fame grew steadily.

Being neither militia nor army, the independent-minded Rangers met their equally independent foes—whether Indians, Mexican raiders, outlaws or fence-cutters—on equal terms. "Born in conflict, schooled in cunningness, shrewdness, and lonely self-reliance, the Texas Rangers created for themselves a tradition in manner, dress, and character," wrote the late Colonel Homer Garrison, Jr. in 1965.

The seven Rangers in this volume—along with countless others— each made a special contribution to the Ranger tradition and to Texas history during the early days of the organization. Although immediate survival might depend upon riding harder and shooting faster than the men they sought, the maintenance of law and order depended on developing a tradition for effective law enforcement.

This tradition is so much a part of Texas history that forward-looking men are determined to preserve it permanently through adaptation of the Ranger Force to the changing times.

Today the Rangers are a six-company unit operating under the command of the chief of criminal law enforcement of the Texas Department of Public Safety, with a captain in command of each company.

The Ranger Force is a group of highly-skilled criminal investigators, composed at this writing of 62 men who are responsible for the prevention, investigation and solution of those offenses falling into the major crime category. In the conduct of his duties, a Ranger may be required to travel by automobile, airplane, helicopter, motorboat, jeep, or on horseback, depending upon the locality and the necessity. Although his basic assignment is within a given area of the state, he may continue an investigation to any part of Texas, and, with the approval of the director of the Department of Public Safety, to any part of the United States.

The Ranger Force of today is specifically charged with these major duties: protection of life and property from violence; suppression of riots and insurrection; apprehension of fugitives; investigation of major crimes such as murder, rape, robbery, burglary, livestock thefts, felonious assaults, and other felonies.

The modern-day Ranger is equipped with and trained in the use of the most modern tools available to law enforcement, including the full facilities of the Texas Department of Public Safety, including the up-to-date crime laboratory and massive criminal record files.

"Texas Ranger" is a title that symbolizes determined and dedicated law enforcement as much today as it did when the Ranger Force was created.

The following statement, uttered many years ago by an early-day Texas Ranger, comes as close as any other to explaining the basic creed of the oldest state law enforcement group on the North American continent—and the philosophy has not changed in more than a century and a half:

> "No man in the wrong can stand up against a man in the right who keeps on a-comin'."

As Director of the Texas Department of Public Safety and Chief of the Texas Rangers, I am proud of the valiant deeds of those pioneer Rangers whose intrepid spirit contributed so greatly to Texas history.

I am also proud to say to the people of Texas that the present-day Texas Ranger Force is upholding the same basic traditions created by their predecessors and at the same time is making perhaps an even greater contribution to this great State in the preservation of law and order. The challenges the Texas Rangers face today, in these times of great technological change, of burgeoning urbanization and industrialization, are being met with modern methods and techniques.

The Texas Rangers are effective not only because they are symbolic of strong and fearless law enforcement and therefore command respect, but because they are equipped with the modern-day capability to cope with the criminal law enforcement problems of the space age.

Wilson E. Speir

Introduction

Of all agencies maintaining law and order in Texas the Rangers have been most successful. When Texas defied the Mexican dictator Santa Anna and a war for independence began, every man was needed to fight the Mexicans, but unfriendly Indians also posed a constant threat. Only a few men could be spared to meet the Indians, and these men would have to cover a vast expanse of territory.

Hence the Permanent Council, the first provisional government of the revolting colonists, authorized Silas M. Parker (later killed by Indians) to employ and direct the activities of twenty-five Rangers whose business should be to "range" and guard the frontier between the Brazos and the Trinity Rivers. The Council also authorized twenty-five volunteer Rangers to "range" between the Colorado and the Brazos Rivers "on the frontier settlements," and thirty-five to guard the country east of the Trinity River. The Consultation, a more representative body that succeeded the Permanent Council, extended the Ranger territory westward to the Guadalupe River. A little later the Texan government provided for a Corps of Rangers, under the command of a major, to consist of three companies of fifty-six men each with a captain and a first and a second lieutenant. Privates were to be enlisted for one year. All were to furnish their own horses, equipment, and munitions.

The word Ranger was not new in Texas at this time. As early as 1823 Austin had employed ten Rangers to protect the colonists, and there are accounts of volunteers doing the work of Rangers in other emergencies. It was, nevertheless, during the Revolution that Texas Rangers began to make a record of public service that has been generally continuous, effective, and often spectacular.

The history of law enforcement on the Texas frontier is largely a history of the Texas Rangers. The reputation of the organization was such, furthermore, that it was not brought to an end with the passing of frontier conditions but has been perpetuated even to our own day as an agency to aid peace officers in suppressing serious crime and dealing with dangerous public disturbances. The plan of this book is to follow a sketch of Texas Rangers through 134 years of history with a study in depth of the lives of seven great Rangers: John Coffee (Jack) Hays and Samuel Walker, Rangers of the Republic and early statehood; Benjamin McCulloch, Ranger and renowned Confederate general; John Salmon (Rip) Ford, Ranger, statesman, editor and Confederate colonel; John B. Jones and Leander H. McNelly, great Ranger commanders of the 1870's; and Lawrence Sullivan Ross, Texas Ranger and governor. Some notable moments in the lives of these men will be portrayed in color.

The unique qualities of Texas Rangers appear in the bands of the Revolution. They were highly mobile, operated in small groups, with little regard for drill and conventional military tactics. Even discipline, as generally understood by men in uniform, was relatively unimportant in contrast with courage, initiative, and self-reliance. The Ranger had to be a good rider and know how to care for his horse. His horse, moreover, was his own property and to neglect it meant loss to himself. A Ranger had to know the country where he ranged and find his way without maps. Marksmanship and the care of arms and munitions were matters of life and death. His enemies were masters of woodcraft and the lore of the plains, and a Ranger had to match their skill and knowledge.

During the Revolution the Rangers made a creditable start. They afforded a modicum of protection from marauding Indians; they aided the people in their flight before the advancing Mexican armies; and to a limited extent they scouted the trails and heralded the approach of Mexican forces. Many years later Ranger Noah Smithwick related some stirring stories of these trying days, one being an incident near Bastrop when the renowned patriot and Ranger commander Major Robert M. Williamson had to be reminded that he had forgotten to call in a sentry before he began a hurried retreat. Smithwick volunteered to return for the sentry, an oldish man, whom he found sitting on a log, a bottle of whiskey beside him, and unperturbed at the report that the Mexicans were at hand.

The outstanding feat of Rangers in the Revolution was that of Captain Isaac Burton and his band of twenty who were ordered to scour the coast in the vicinity of Copano Bay to prevent the landing of supplies for the Mexican army. Although in the beginning they did not have a boat of any sort, they succeeded by a series of ruses and audacious moves in capturing three vessels with supplies valued at $25,000, and were dubbed "The Horse Marines."

Rangers had an increasing share in defending the Republic of Texas. Sam Houston, the first constitutional president, sought to keep all expenditures at a minimum. Accordingly, he dismissed the greater part of the army by furlough and left to Rangers the main task of defense. Several laws authorized riflemen or other volunteer forces tantamount to Texas Rangers, but the laws were put into effect only partially. One role, somewhat unique for Rangers was that of Noah Smithwick during this period when he went as emissary to a Comanche Indian village, sojourned with the Indians for some weeks, and apparently brought about peace for a season with at least one Comanche band. More dramatic was the expedition of a small force led by Lieutenant A. B. Benthusen of the Mounted Gunmen and Captain William Eastland of the Rangers which resulted in desperate fighting with Indians far in the interior, on the Trinity River above the site of Dallas. This episode occurred in October, 1837.

During the three-year presidency of Mirabeau B. Lamar, who succeeded Houston in December 1838, wars between the settlers and Indians became the normal relationship. The Indians were resisting the encroachment on their country by the white people and, moreover, found marauding more profitable and interesting than a monotonous life of peace. Mounted Volunteers, aggregating nearly five hundred men rank and file, took the field with several companies of Rangers. All were in effect Rangers: that is they were enlisted for a relatively short period, to be used principally for frontier protection, each man to provide his own horse and equipment. They would, furthermore, operate in small units.

In these wars with Indians, the Rangers were in the van of the fighting. Captain John Bird lost his life in a fight with Indians near the site of Temple. Colonel John H. Moore commanding a Ranger force defeated severely a band of Comanches on the upper Colorado River. A band of seventeen Rangers, under the command of Lieutenant James O. Rice, killed Manuel Flores, a Mexican spy, and found on his body papers revealing a plan to unite Indians and Mexicans in a general war against Texas.

Texas Rangers shared in defeating a large body of Comanches at Plum Creek, near the site of Lockhart, on August 12, 1840. Ben McCulloch and John Coffee (Jack) Hays were there, and the Texans likely used a revolver that had been perfected by the manufacturer Samuel Colt to meet the specifications given him by the Texas Ranger Samuel Walker.

It was during the War with Mexico, 1846-1848, that Texas Rangers first became nationally known. They were represented by two regiments called Mounted Volunteers, commanded by Colonels Jack Hays and George T. Wood. Hays' regiment, made up principally of volunteers from West Texas, had in it many men seasoned in warfare with Indians and Mexicans. Wherever they went Texas Rangers attracted attention. A contemporary described Jack Hays' regiment thus:

> men in groups with long beards and mustaches, dressed in every variety of garment, with one exception, the slouched hat and unmistakable uniform of a Texas Ranger, and a belt of pistols around their waists . . . a rougher looking set we never saw. . . . Notwithstanding their ferocious and outlaw look, there were among them doctors and lawyers, and many a college graduate. . . .

And he added that they appeared to be "an orderly and well-mannered people."

Texans had hoped that after annexation the might of the United States government would restrain the Indians along the northern frontier and lawless characters along the Rio Grande. Hence, for a period the state did little in the way of frontier defense. The federal government took over its responsibilities in Texas tardily, constructing two cordons of military posts from the Rio Grande to the upper Brazos and Trinity Rivers and strengthening the defense along the Rio Grande. Unfortunately the troops placed in these far-flung forts were largely infantrymen, as helpless in combating mounted Indians as a latter-day foot patrolman would be in dealing with speed-law violators. Federal Indian agents sought to control and protect their charges, and on land given by the state, the federal Indian service established two reservations for Indians on the upper Brazos River. Many of the Indians refused to enter the reservations and continued to live by marauding, however, and the frontier people kept up their march into the Indians' hunting grounds. Hense, the confusion along the frontier and the inadequate force of mounted troops made it necessary for the army to call on the Rangers for aid.

The frontier settlers also often urged that Rangers be used. Five companies of 79 men each were called out for a short period in 1850, and such names as John Salmon Ford, Big Foot Wallace, and Henry McCulloch appear in the list of officers. Serving for short periods, using their own horses and to a degree their own arms and equipment, these men were often called mounted volunteers or minute men, but they were essentially Rangers. Their efforts were directly mainly to protecting frontier counties against depredating Indians, but one emergency company gave special protection to Mexican teamsters on the road between Port LaVaca and San Antonio.

In 1858 Texas Rangers caught the attention of Texas, and indeed of the nation. Texans were disgruntled at the failure of the general government to protect the frontier, and Governor Runnels made John S. Ford senior captain to command all state forces and bring peace. In a daring campaign Ford asserted the authority of Texas over a considerable part of the Indian Territory and defeated a large arrogant Comanche band. A similar feat was that of Lawrence Sullivan Ross, who commanded 125 Texas Reservation Indians in company with Major Earl Van Dorn and his troops of the Second United States Cavalry and Fifth Infantry and beat the Comanches again in a severe fight north of the Red River.

Notwithstanding the loyal aid given the troops and Rangers by the Texas Reservation Indians, they were charged, unjustly in most cases, with depredations committed by Indians that had never accepted life on the reservation. Hostility against them mounted. Ford and his Rangers could not protect them from the fury of white frontiersmen, and for their own safety they were removed to a reservation in the Indian Territory. Thereafter Indians in Texas were trespassers, generally regarded as outlaws and when they visited the state they sustained that reputation.

When he became governor of Texas in 1859, Sam Houston made much use of Rangers. He called out and placed along the frontier nearly a thousand and sent a formidable force into the Indian country under the veteran Ranger M. T. Johnson—all with little result. It seems that for awhile Houston thought of Texas Rangers as the nucleus of an Anglo-American force to occupy and bring order to Mexico. During this period warfare prevailed between Mexicans and Anglo-Americans along the lower Rio Grande, and out of the struggle emerged the hero and bandit Juan N. Cortinas. Rangers shared with the United States Army the credit of bringing these disturbances to a halt.

Although their relative importance diminished during the Civil War because of the increasing numbers of other military forces, the Texas Rangers carried on. A Frontier Regiment, commanded at first by Colonel James M. Norris and later by Colonel J. E. McCord guarded the frontier of Northwest Texas. Although it probably had the poorest of arms, munitions, and supplies to be found in any fighting aggregation from the Rio Grande to the Atlantic Ocean, it did its task about as well as the stronger and better equipped forces that had preceded it.

A renowned organization during the Civil War was Terry's Texas Rangers, a regiment of volunteers mustered in at Houston on September 9, 1861, through the efforts of Benjamin F. Terry and Thomas S. Lubbock. Officially it became the 8th Texas Cavalry, Confederate States of America, but it retained the Texas Ranger name and stamp throughout more than three years of warfare in such battles as Shilough, Murfreesboro, Chickamauga, and Knoxville.

Like the Ranger organizations that preceded it, Terry's regiment was observed with keen interest wherever it went; and there was much comment, no little of it unfavorable.

> From the standpoint of the martinet [wrote L. B. Giles, a member] our organization could hardly be called a regiment. A distinguished lieutenant general is reported as saying that it was not a regiment at all but a 'd - 'd armed mob.' If there was every any serious attempt to discipline it, the effort was soon abandoned. . . . To our credit it may be said that few ever avoided a fight. There were few real cowards among us and they were simply objects of pity.

Terry's men were superb horsemen, generally well mounted and well armed, and on a score of fields they proved their valor and effectiveness in battle.

Texans sought to reestablish the Ranger force immediately after the Civil War, but the federal authorities would not permit it. A State Police force. which operated from July 1870 till April 1873 was both ineffective and unpopular. The practice of Governor E. J. Davis of declaring martial law in certain counties and enforcing his decrees with State Police maintained at county expense was highly obnoxious. Beginning with early 1874 conservative Democrats again controlled the legislature and Richard Coke, a Confederate veteran, was governor. One of the first acts of the new regime was to create anew the Ranger organization.

The need for such a force was never greater. The war had impoverished the state and reconstruction had disorganized its society. Along the frontier and even in some relatively populous communities criminals had joined Civil War deserters and conscription dodgers, and with thousands of men crime and lawlessness had become a habit. The adjutant general's list of wanted men exceeded 3,000. Lawless elements had taken over entire counties and local officers were unable to assert the authority of the state. Many officers were cowed; not a few were venal. Feudists not only waylaid their enemies but not infrequently assassinated witnesses.

Along the Rio Grande, extending at times far into the interior, marauders from Mexico wrought destruction. In Northwest Texas the extension of the cattlemen's frontier after the ending of the Indian menace in the middle 1870's added greatly to the problem of law enforcement. The frontier had been a relatively narrow band extending from the Rio Grande to the Red River across the center of the state. Now, it was widened in the course of a year or two so that the isolated camps of the cattlemen were scattered from the Rolling Plains to the Pecos and beyond. Regular local government was not organized in this region for several years and the need for a special agency to assert the authority of the state became imperative.

Rangers fit such situations remarkably well. They were not limited by county boundaries: they could move as one man or as thirty; and they could be independent of local voters and local influence.

One law enacted in 1874 established a "Special Force" of Rangers to deal with banditry on the Mexican border of the lower Rio Grande, another authorized the Frontier Battalion, designed primarily to suppress attacks by Indians, but destined to attain greater renown as the suppressor of banditry and rule by mobs. Captain L. H. McNelly, a member of General Thomas Green's staff during the Civil War, commanded the Special Force of Rangers, and Major John B. Jones, a Civil War captain, commanded the Frontier Battalion. The soft-spoken McNelly brought a measure of security to several feud-ridden, bandit-infested South Texas counties. In directing and leading his Frontier Battalion, the quiet and unassuming Jones had an important share in bringing to an end the Indian menace and in suppressing lawlessness generally.

Rangers had to be versatile and equal to many sorts of tasks. For instance, Captain George W. Arrington drove away Indians from the Texas Panhandle as the cattlemen were taking over the country and brought a measure of law and order to such new crossroads centers as Mobeetie, Tascosa, Fort Elliott, Fort Griffin, and Doan's on the Red River. During this period in far West Texas Rangers George W. Baylor, James B. Gillett, and C. L. Nevill were meeting the threats of Apaches and outlaws.

Rangers were equally effective in the organized counties where the supremacy of the law was threatened. Any Ranger could make an arrest, escort prisoners, and guard jails. One Ranger might even suppress a mob or strengthen the spine of a wavering judge or sheriff. If more were needed, generally they could be had.

The distinguished historian Walter Prescott Webb stated that the Frontier Battalion should have been brought to an end immediately after the death of Major John B. Jones in 1881. This was not because of the death of Jones but because the work of the organization had been completed. Its purpose had been primarily to protect the frontier people from Indians, Mexicans, and outlaws in regions where the local forces of the law were too weak and far-flung to prevail against these enemies. Now conditions had changed. The Indian menace had been brought to an end and there were local forces to deal with other problems. At about this time, furthermore, several outstanding Ranger officers resigned, among them Lee Hall, who had suppressed the Sutton-Taylor feud; Dan W. Roberts, a great Indian fighter; John B. Armstrong, captor of the outlaw John Wesley Hardin; C. L. Nevill, enemy of marauding Indians and horse thieves; and George W. Baylor, who destroyed the last of Victorio's Apache band.

The last two decades of the twentieth century brought plenty of work for the Texas Rangers, nevertheless. Foreign capitalists, along with citizens of the country who had the means, bought and fenced large ranches. This practice "fenced out" numbers of little cattlemen who did not own the lands they had been using and did not have the money to buy them. Some of them resisted by cutting the fences. Soon fence-cutting became an epidemic in a band of counties across the center of the state, and in many communities sentiment on the subject was so divided that local peace officers could not or would not stop the practice or even arrest those who perpetrated it. In many communities the burden of suppressing it was on the Rangers. Captain L. P. Sieker, Quartermaster of the Frontier Battalion directed such staunch enemies of crime as Sergeant Ira Aten in suppressing the practice and bringing an end to the craze.

Rangers continued to be the arm of the government most feared by train and bank robbers. They asserted the authority of the state in preventing a prize fight in El Paso in 1896, and at times they met with moderate success in the most difficult task of enforcing quarantine regulations along the Rio Grande border. In 1893 Captain Frank Jones was killed in suppressing disorders on Pirate Island, apparently a sort of no-man's land in the Rio Grande in the El Paso region.

An opinion of Attorney General T. S. Smith May 26, 1900, in reply to an inquiry by Governor Joseph D. Sayers, reduced drastically the powers of the Frontier Battalion. The law of 1874 authorizing the battalion read that each officer of the organization should have all the powers of a peace officer, that is the authority of making arrests. Rangers had acted on the assumption that each Ranger was an officer, and their success had been made possible largely because every man in the organization might in effect exercise these powers. Now only Ranger officers could make arrests and the rank and file of the men could act only as their assistants.

The decision threatened the existence of the organization, but a second opinion of the attorney general made possible a temporary reorganization and a law became effective July 8, 1901, creating a new Ranger force much like the old. Its purpose was for protecting the frontier against marauding or thieving parties and for the suppression of lawlessness and crime throughout the state. Arms were similar to those of other years, and the men were to supply their own horses. There was to be no uniform or badge. Captains might choose their own men, taking care that they were courageous, discreet, honest, temperate and of good families. There were to be four companies of not more than twenty men with a captain and a sergeant each.

The reduced force maintained the Ranger tradition quite well. Captain James A. Brooks and a few companions suppressed cattle theft in the King Ranch vicinity on the lower Gulf Coast. Captain John R. Hughes and his little company gave some protection to El Paso in 1911 when the Mexican Revolution, with Pancho Villa just across the Rio Grande, imperiled the people of that region. As the revolution beyond the Rio Grande proceeded, confusion and violence increased on both sides of the river. At points from El Paso to Brownsville trains were robbed, persons were kidnaped, and scores of people were killed. When the United States entered World War I in April, 1917, German spies joined other trouble-makers. For a while Ranger Charles S. Stevens spent most of his time searching for and arresting persons suspected of espionage.

As conditions grew more confused and violence increased, the little force of regular Rangers was woefully inadequate for border defense and was increased to 1,000 men, most of them stationed on the border. In enlistments the spoils system prevailed, there was little screening, and the quality of the force deteriorated rapidly with the great inrush of novices. Charges of Ranger brutality brought a legislative investigation. A law of March 31, 1919, reduced the Rangers to four companies not exceeding fifteen privates each with a small contingent of officers.

The most widely known Texas Ranger near the turn of the century was William Jesse (Bill) McDonald. As deputy sheriff, special Ranger, and United States marshal, McDonald had made a reputation as tamer of cattle thieves, train robbers and frontier bullies in North Texas, No Man's Land, and the Cherokee Strip when Governor James S. Hogg made his captain of Company B, Frontier Battalion in 1894. He soon became linked with breaking up a nest of cattle thieves in Hutchinson County, capturing bank robbers, and solving murder mysteries. He became widely known through such appearances as being special officer at the Democratic "Car Stable" convention at Houston in 1892, bodyguard for President Theodore Roosevelt in Texas, and (after his Ranger career had ended) bodyguard for President Woodrow Wilson. He was a remarkable detective and it was said of him that he had the "eyes of a fox, ears of a wolf, and could follow a scent like a hound."

During the twentieth century newly-established oil towns often needed the attention of Rangers. Within weeks following a discovery a cross-roads hamlet or village might become a teeming city of thousands. Conditions would get beyond the control of local officials and lawlessness and crime would prevail. Then the Rangers would be sent in, and they often laid a heavy hand on criminals in Ranger, Breckenridge, Desdemona, Borger, Kilgore, and several other communities. Often there were no city jails, and it was necessary to chain prisoners to telephone poles for short periods, a practice that brought forth sharp criticism.

A widely-known Texas Ranger of the twentieth century was Frank Hamer. He attracted public attention in 1928 by his fight against the Texas Bankers' Association practice of paying a reward of $5,000 for each dead bank robber. He contended that the rewards had resulted in a vicious racket whereby certain villainous men enticed weak novices in crime into bank robberies in order to have them killed for the reward. Hamer became even more widely known in 1934 when he ended the career of the bandit Clyde Barrow (charged with fifteen murders) and his companion Bonnie Parker.

In 1935 the legislature made a drastic change in the Texas Rangers, reducing the force to two mounted companies and a headquarters company aggregating forty men. The law made the force a part of the Texas Department of Public Safety, linking it with the Highway Patrol of 140 men at that time. The prediction that the new arrangement would prove the beginning of the end of the Texas Rangers has not come to pass. The force was still needed; indeed subsequent legislatures have deemed it indispensable.

In 1969 the Rangers consist of sixty-two men, including six captains and six sergeants, divided into six companies, located in different parts of the state. They are charged with a variety of duties: the protection of life and property; the suppression of riots and insurrections; the apprehension of fugitives; and the transporting of prisoners. Emphasis is placed on cooperating with local peace officers in investigating major crimes. Every Ranger is a detective.

For obvious reasons the Rangers' means of travel and their equipment have changed. They travel mainly in cars equipped with three-way radios, but at times they go by plane, by boat, on horseback, or on foot with walkie-talkies. They are equipped with pistols, rifles, shotguns, tear-gas guns, grenades, and gas masks. Still they hold on to several links with the past: they do not wear uniforms; and each Ranger is required always to have a horse available for immediate use, for their work may take them away from roads and trails.

The record of "the oldest law enforcing agency in North America with statewide jurisdiction" has not been without blemish. Charges of unwarranted severity and needless killings have been made and not without foundation. In contrast, there are cases where Rangers have shown admirable restraint and, at their own peril, have been generous with criminals.

Since they shielded frontier settlers from Comanche spears and arrows and helped the terrified colonists cross swollen streams during the Runaway Scrape, Texas Rangers have come a long way. They gave some sense of security to the people of the Texas Republic and made both Indians and Mexicans know that the fighters of the little nation could be dangerous; and when the state was young, Rangers audaciously went beyond its borders to suppress marauders.

The Texas Ranger force has been primarily a civil, not a military, aggregation. Yet Ranger units shared heavily in the taking of Monterrey and Mexico City, and one regiment fought for the Confederacy in half a dozen states. Texas feudists and wire cutters could not always be suppressed, but the presence of Rangers restrained the lawless and gave courage to the men of good will who opposed them. Along with the cattlemen of the open range, Rangers crossed swollen streams, faced hail and lightning, rode in winds that burned their faces and northers that chilled their bones to drive out Indians and suppress crime. If at times they were not able to bring law and order to the Rio Grande border their presence was a threat to criminals and their spectacular feats helped by calling the attention of the nation to the problem. Texas Rangers have added much to the Texas heritage, and it is fitting that their memory be preserved in the life stories of seven of the greatest. It is gratifying, moreover, to know that the organization still carries on.

Rupert N. Richardson

David Sanders

Art connoisseurs in Texas and the Southwest will be delighted with the artist featured in this book. He is David Sanders, one of the better-known artists in Texas. His portrait work, landscapes, and country scenes are highly acclaimed in the art circles of Texas where he has taught and exhibited on numerous occasions. *The Rangers of Texas,* however, is allowing Sanders to display his favorite art theme: Western Americana.

His desire to capture the American scene as authentically as possible has led David Sanders to travel extensively throughout the Southwest. During his trips, he visits and sketches the Indians and panorama of Texas, Arizona and New Mexico. The sketches later became the subjects of his popular Western paintings.

Although David Sanders began to paint at the age of ten while still living in his native San Antonio, Texas, he has come to be a free-lance artist in a most round-about manner. The detour began while he was attending Alamo Heights High School where he took a special liking to both art and music. Throughout high school he also studied art at the Witte Memorial Museum of San Antonio. Meanwhile, he earned his expense money by singing semi-professionally.

Although already a promising artist, David enrolled at San Antonio Junior College to study music. Upon completion of two years of study there, he went to work full time and supplemented his income by painting and singing. In 1957, David joined the Army and served in Okinawa where he also managed to study music. After completing his military obligation, he studied and worked in Seattle for two years before returning to San Antonio.

In 1963, Sanders decided to return to college to obtain a degree. Thus he enrolled at Southwest Texas State University at San Marcos. Surprisingly, though, he majored in commercial art. Also while at San Marcos, David married the former Miss Sally Todd, his college sweetheart. The Sanders have two children—Sarah Kathleen (1965), and David Lawrence (1967).

Ever since his college graduation in 1965, David Sanders has been a free-lance artist. Moreover, he has conducted art classes in Seguin, Llano and New Braunfels. Success, however, has not changed the quiet, modest artist who as a rule does not enter competitive art shows. Two exceptions to this rule have been the San Antonio River Art Show where he won the Joskes award, and the Waco Brazos River Art Festival. Most important, it was the Waco Festival that brought him to the attention of Texian Press which then commissioned him to illustrate *The Rangers of Texas*.

Drawing strongly from his personal knowledge of the Texas topography, David succeeded in capturing the color and mood of each of the Ranger scenes. Nonetheless, he insisted on visiting as many of the actual sites as possible in order to recreate the scenes authentically. The dress, weapons and descriptions of the events were drawn from the memoirs, eye-witness accounts and period paintings. It is thus with great pleasure that Texian Press presents the authentically recreated events in the lives of some of the most outstanding Rangers of Texas.

The Paintings

Jack (Coffee) Hays at Enchanted Rock, August 1841, is depicted the moment the Comanche Indians finally decided to attack after threatening to do so for some two hours. Having separated himself from a Ranger scouting expedition, Hays climbed Enchanted Rock where he suddenly found himself surrounded by the Comanche. He simultaneously discovered that he had lost or forgotten his powder horn and ammunition. He had only eleven shots and a Bowie knife to defend himself. No one fired until that tense moment, now captured on canvas, when the Comanche finally advanced amidst a chorus of war-whoops.

Capt. Ben McCulloch at Encarnacion, February 1847, captures these quiet minutes for which the two Ranger scouts had been awaiting in order to ascertain the strength of the Mexican Army on the field. Quickly, with a coolness matching that of the morning breeze, Ben McCulloch and his partner scrutinized the scene below them. The intelligence coup was to be of great value to General Scott's command and a most decisive incident in the outcome of his Mexican campaign.

Samuel Walker, October 1847, depicts the excitement, glory and color of a cavalry charge during the U.S.-Mexican War. The scene is the quiet and obscure town of Humantla where a Mexican artillery contingent stood between the Rangers and Santa Anna. The Rangers were thus doubly eager to overrun the position and capture their arch enemy. The full tension of the scene is captured in those eternal seconds immediately prior to the initial contact. The frightened artilleryman ready to use his ramrod as a club, the cavalry officer being shot off his saddle, and the reckless determination of the Ranger charge is depicted in all its splendor.

John S. (Rip) Ford at the Canadian River, May 12, 1858, is depicted during those restrained moments when the Rangers and Indian allies confronted Comanche Chief Iron Jacket. The chief, wearing an antiquated

Spanish coat-of-mail, daringly rode up to the Ranger entourage and hurled insults at them. The defiant, if not-too-wise Iron Jacket considered himself immortal. One of Rip Ford's Rangers, being not too patient but even less credulous of the Chief's immortality, shot and killed the Comanche.

Sul Ross and Peta Nocona, December, 1860, captures the savage nobility of the dying Indian chief who asked no quarter. Brutal in his warrior days, the old chief and father of Quanah Parker stands alone and mortally wounded, awaiting the arrival of death. Looking directly and unafraid at Sul Ross, the old chief sings the death chant of his people. He is defiantly oblivious to all the destruction about him. Perhaps in mutual respect for a worthy and noble opponent, Sul Ross chose not to personally put Peta Nocona out of his misery. Instead, the Ranger instructed his Mexican companion to finish the old chief.

Lee H. McNelly on Border Patrol, 1875, is depicted along the banks of the Rio Grande in the Big Bend area. The keen apprehension of the Ranger patrol as it surveys every inch in sight searching for smugglers and Mexican bandits is realistically captured. The magnificent and breath-taking beauty of the Big Bend, with the quietly flowing Rio Grande serve to portray the tension and ominous splendor of the scene. The border patrols served to instill the long-standing fear and hatred of the Rangers along the Rio Grande.

John B. Jones at Round Rock, July 19, 1878 is shown the day he literally ended the flambouyant career of Sam Bass. The outlaw and four of his men had entered the town to prepare for a bank robbery, not knowing one of their number had informed the Rangers. When first approached in Kopperel's General Merchandise Store the outlaws quickly shot and killed one deputy and disabled another. The scene that followed is then captured on canvas as Sam Bass, already wounded, and two of his men make for their horses. Ranger Jones, his deputies and some citizens are hot in pursuit of the would-be bank robbers. Sam Bass was mortally wounded and died three days later.

RICHARD G. SANTOS
Archivist of Bexar County
Office of County Clerk

Acknowledgments

Texian Press wishes to thank the following people who contributed to the publication of this volume: The authors who always find time to write and research the articles; David Sanders who spent unlimited hours in capturing on canvas the realism of the events; Colonel Wilson Spier, Director of the Department of Public Safety for his excellent and timely foreword; as always, Richard G. Santos could be counted on for research and writing about the paintings; Dr. Rupert N. Richardson's introduction brings together much of the total history of the Texas Rangers; Fred Jones and Billy Don Shirley who labored well to transfer the manuscripts into type; Frances Haynes and Darlene Tindell who read proofs; Earl Ray Davis II, Mike Prim, Ray Badley, E. R. Davis and J. B. Davis helped in every way with this production; Travis Lawson for his overall help in production. To all of the above we say thanks.

TEXIAN PRESS

Table of Contents

John Coffee Hays 5

Samuel H. Walker 31

Ben McCulloch 61

John Salmon (Rip) Ford 81

Lawrence Sullivan Ross 111

Leander H. McNelly 131

John B. Jones 147

John Coffee Hays

Jack Hays on Enchanted Rock -- Fall of 1841

John Coffee Hays

by

DORMAN H. WINFREY

John Coffee Hays, better known in Texas as Jack Hays, has been characterized as the most spectacular and successful Indian fighter in Texas history. A man who rarely engaged less than ten and occasionally forty times his own number but was never defeated was once described by rancher S. M. Swenson as "the only fighter God ever made."

Republic of Texas President Sam Houston said, "You may rely on the gallant Hays and his companions." Flacco of the Lipans described Hays in these words: "Captain Jack heap brave; not afraid to go to hell by himself." Biographer James K. Greer wrote, "Jack Hays's name heads the list of those who created the [Texas Ranger] tradition," and historian Walter Prescott Webb wrote in his study of the oldest law enforcement body in the world that under Jack Hays's leadership "the best tradition of the Texas Rangers was established." As a Texas Ranger Jack Hays became a legend during the thirteen years he lived in Texas and had the unusual distinction of earning an illustrious reputation after moving to California—first as a sheriff and later as a developer of the city of Oakland.

The popularity of Jack Hays during his lifetime was rather remarkable because he never sought fame or honor. Unlike some early Texas frontiersmen, he did not wear a snakeskin vest, drink hard liquor, or swear. He showed himself wise, courageous, and sometimes daring and brash, but never for the aim of fame. Hays was good-natured and without vanity. Though involved in the most publicly acclaimed events, he exhibited great diffidence in the glare of public attention. His contemporary John S. Ford recalled that Hays blushed when confronted with a compliment. As an older man in Oakland, Hays was said to go to town in a buggy rather than on horseback to escape the glare of public attention.

Widely respected and liked, he was much admired for his temperate attitude, the more so as it contrasted so strongly with the generally prevalent one among the rank and file of the Rangers. His popularity grew not only from a liking for heroes; it was also a recognition of something substantial in the character of the man.

In appearance Hays seems to have been an enigma of his contemporaries, who thought he did not sufficiently look the part of a western fighter. Standing five feet eight or nine inches tall and weighing about 150 pounds, with reddish brown hair and hazel eyes, he seemed not at all what one might expect of the most renowned Indian and outlaw fighter of his day.

Hays's character drew its strength from deeper roots than outward swagger. Other members of his family demonstrated the same qualities that he himself possessed. His grandfather, John Hays, an Irish immigrant who settled in Rockbridge County, Virginia, had served as a major under Mad Anthony Wayne during the Revolutionary War. Later he was an officer under General Andrew Jackson in the Creek War, as was Jack's father, Harmon. Jack's brother Harry became a general in the Confederate Army.

Born on January 28, 1817, at Little Cedar Lick in Wilson County, Tennessee, Jack grew up in the area that boasted such men as Sam Houston and Andrew Jackson. The fact that Mrs. Andrew Jackson was his father's aunt probably provided him with an entry to many places in his later life. Until his sixteenth year, Jack lived a near-ideal existence among the forests and fields of Middle Tennessee. It was said that even at this early age he had mastered riding and shooting—the skills which were to make him famous—and at running his speed was exceptional. When Jack was sixteen, this idyllic life ended, for his parents were stricken with yellow fever and died within a few days of each other. Following this tragedy, Hays and a younger brother and sister were taken by an uncle to live on his plantation in Mississippi. Here Jack remained until he was nineteen.

On arriving at his uncle's home, young Hays decided to learn surveying as a profession and hired himself out as a chain carrier. Soon he was being employed by land speculators to locate lands for them. After continuing this pursuit for two years, Hays saved enough money to afford a year's study at Davidson Academy in Nashville. Apparently even at this age he had his heart set on a military career, for he evidently tried to persuade his uncle to send him to West Point. His uncle resisted this request, and perhaps his doing so was the prime motive in turning Hays toward the new land of Texas. Certainly opportunities for a militarily inclined man abounded there; but whatever his reasons— whether to find military adventure or to lessen his uncle's responsibility for the orphaned children—in 1836 Hays left the security of his relatives' home in Mississippi and turned toward the dangers of a new life in Texas. Traveling by way of New Orleans, he fell in with a group of ninety volunteers from Kentucky, Mississippi, and Louisiana—like himself on their way to Texas—and traveled with them to Nacogdoches, where he first entered the soil where he was to win his greatest reputation.

For the first time, in 1836, the people of Texas knew what it was to have the responsibility for their own destiny. Under the Mexican Republic, the Anglo population had been privileged to adopt a negative stance—against tyranny, against injustice, against Mexico. Now Texans had to construct a future, and that was not easy. It was natural that uncertainty and fear should rule their lives. In the severe political depression that followed the clash of two civilizations in the Texas Revolution, the early days of the Republic were marked by a pervasive fear of attack. This was not entirely unwarranted, for Mexican and Indian raiders were constant threats on the frontier of the sparsely settled nation. It was in trying to come to grips with these encroachments that Jack Hays would spend nearly a decade of his life.

Upon arriving in Texas soon after the Battle of San Jacinto, Hays enlisted as a private in the Texas Army, which at that time was camped on the Brazos under the command of General Felix Huston. For more than two years he was to serve here and in loosely organized "ranging" companies, chiefly as a spy—really a member of a reconnaissance patrol rather than what we consider a "spy" today. Hays's first major assignment after joining the army was to help to bury the remains of Fannin's 350 men; doubtless this duty served to impress upon the youth the nature of the situation he had brought himself into.

Hays was to prove himself highly capable in years to come, but he seems to have gotten his start less through proven ability than through his family's name and its acquaintance with Sam Houston, the President of the Republic. Apparently, when the volunteers were furloughed after San Jacinto while the government attempted to raise the money to pay and discharge them, Hays visited President Houston, who advised him to join a company of rangers being enlisted for service on the southwestern frontier by Erastus (Deaf) Smith. Hays took Houston's advice, and he served under Smith three or four months before transferring to Captain Henry Karnes's company.

At the beginning of 1836 there had been a small ranging force in the field which was later divided into four detachments. But these rangers were not full-time lawmen; rather they were more of a minuteman organization, available to be called up on notice but not always on patrol.

During this time Hays was promoted to sergeant and made at least two reconnaissance trips to the Laredo area—claimed by Texas but still under the flag of Mexico. He proved so troublesome to the Mexicans in the area that General Rafael Vasquez was sent north toward Bexar with orders to liquidate Hays and his small force. Learning that the Mexicans planned to trick him, Hays turned the tables, met Vasquez before the Mexican force was ready to fight, and effectively cleared the area of invaders for the time.

Hays had dismissed his small force when word came in August, 1840, that the Texans were to gather on Plum Creek to intercept a force of Comanches who were returning from their raid at Linnville. The daring raid on Linnville is best remembered because of the participants' recollections of Indians dressed in the clothing they took. Few lives were lost as most of the town's inhabitants managed to escape to boats lying at anchor in the port. The Texans decided that the Indians would probably return to the plains by the same route they had used to reach the coast. Hays was among those who gathered at Plum Creek to meet the Comanches. In the Battle of Plum Creek nearly a hundred Indians were killed without the loss of a Texan.

By 1840 Hays was making a name for himself. In February of that year a group of San Antonio citizens recommended Hays to President Lamar as a candidate to survey the boundary of Travis County, in which Austin had just been located as the capital; they noted that he had been professionally engaged as a surveyor in the county for the past two years. Probably they referred to his employment after the Revolution in surveying government grants to soldiers on the western streams of Texas and in escorting surveying parties. The next year he would be elected county surveyor by the citizens of Bexar County, and several years later, while he was engaged in exploring a route through the Big Bend area of Texas, he received an appointment as district surveyor for the Bexar District.

While his activities were not all military during this time, nonetheless, Hays's life was progressing almost inevitably toward those events which were to win him the renown he still enjoys. He must have demonstrated his outstanding abilities during his service under Smith and Karnes, for shortly after the Battle of Plum Creek in 1840 he received a commission from President Lamar as a captain of his own spy company stationed in San Antonio. This was not yet the company which was to make famous the name of the Texas Rangers, but it served effectively in the area around San Antonio against incursions by Indians and raiders from across the Mexican border.

The real history of the Texas Rangers as they are remembered today began in 1840, when Hays became a captain. Later, in 1842, when Congress authorized the President to accept the services of one company of volunteers to range on the Trinity and Navasota rivers and two companies to range on the southwest frontier, Hays was promoted to the grade of major and assigned to command the two companies on the southwest frontier. San Antonio was the official headquarters of Hays's company, although most of the time it was camped on the Medina. Many of the men who served under Hays were to win fame at least as great as that of their leader: Ben McCulloch, his second in command; Henry E. McCulloch; William A. A. (Bigfoot) Wallace; and Peter Hansborough Bell, later governor.

Hays had extraordinary authority; he could declare martial law in the territory he patroled; and, judging from his actions, he could summarily execute captured felons. His duties were not restricted to keeping the peace; he was also given the responsibility for exchanging prisoners of war with Mexico and was authorized by Sam Houston to "adopt the proper means" for reestablishing trade with Mexico. Thus, his men were not strictly keepers of law and order; at least, they were not only that.

On January 23, 1844, Hays's responsibilities increased when Congress authorized him to raise a company of mounted gunmen to act as Rangers on the western and southwestern frontier, from Bexar to Refugio counties and west. On December 14, 1844, H. L. Kinney was further authorized to raise a company for the protection of Corpus Christi. An additional law of February, 1845, extended Hays's authority; he was to have charge of four companies stationed along the frontier from Refugio and Goliad counties to Robertson and Milam and was to command at Bexar. The officers of these companies were to "scour the frontiers of their respective counties, protect them from incursions, and when concentrated in emergencies, to be under the command of Captain Hays."

It was said at the time, and believed, that "one Ranger was worth five or six Indians." This came to be true, but not for reasons of superior skill or courage, as is sometimes implied. Indeed, the Comanches, on whom Hays expended most of his men's energies, were among the most courageous and skilled of cavalry fighters. Their tactics were far from primitive and—combined with their advantage of fighting on their native territory—made them more than a match for the Rangers, but for one thing: their weapons. The Indians were armed only with bows and arrows, sometimes supported by a lance and a shield capable of warding off a musket ball.

When the Rangers first came into the field, the two combatants were almost equally matched; the Ranger had a long and clumsy rifle, and sometimes a shotgun and a single-shot pistol. The rifle and shotgun were impossible to use from a mounted position with any accuracy, making it necessary to dismount each time they were fired, a great handicap. Furthermore, the muzzle-loading rifle required a minute for an expert to load and probably longer under battle conditions—they were accurate, though, when not fired from the back of a horse. Against these weapons the Indians had developed a very effective tactic, which at the same time worked ideally against the Texans' usual strategy: to ride to the scene of battle, leave their horses under guard, and move on foot to the attack. The Indians soon learned to circle the dismounted Texans, wait until they had fired their rifles, and then move in for the kill. The Texans attempted to counter this move by dividing their forces into squads, each firing at different times so that they were never entirely without firepower. However, this maneuver demanded a disciplined body of men, which the Texas Rangers were not.

With the coming of the revolver, however, the balance of power was radically shifted. The Colt revolver was a five-shot cap and ball of .36 caliber and seven and one-half inch barrel that Hays obtained for his mounted volunteers. Instead of the three or four shots the Texan might be able to fire without reloading, he now could fire thirteen shots without reloading (assuming that in addition to the revolver, he still kept his rifle and pistol). Shortly after the invention of the five-shooter by Samuel Colt, the navy of Texas obtained fifty or sixty of these improved firearms. Subsequently, as it was supposed they were more needed on the frontier than in the navy, they (or at least a portion of them) were turned over to Hays's ranging Company. Their effectiveness was amply demonstrated at the Battle of Walker's Creek in present Kendall County, an encounter in which the Rangers defeated a band of Indians five times their number.

Hays and his fifteen men had camped on the Medina near San Antonio on the night of May 31, 1844. The following morning they set out to search for hostile Indians. About noon, having found no Indians, they returned to Walker's Creek, a dry branch of Sister Creek about three and a half miles from the Guadalupe River in present Kendall County. The men spotted a wild bee colony about thirty feet up a cypress tree, and two of them climbed the tree to steal some honey.

Looking out on the prairie from this vantage point, one of the Rangers saw a small party of Indians watching the proceedings from horseback. Hays then mounted his men, and the party of Comanches, Wacos, and Mexicans fled, perhaps hoping to lead the Texans into an ambush. Hays, however, had no intention of being trapped. Waiting until he saw a line of warriors on a bluff to the north, he then moved to attack them from the rear. The Indians began to encircle the Texans, threatening the small force with annihilation. And they might have done so had it not been for the Rangers' newly acquired five-shooters. Up to this time the Texans could perhaps have driven the Indians away on their first charge, but then they would have had to stop to reload their rifles. This time, the Rangers were each equipped with two five-shooters with two loaded cylinders for each pistol, and the Indians were forced to withdraw first. Hays then decided that the Indians would not return to attack and took the initiative. In the charge that followed, four Texans were severely wounded, one of them mortally. But the Indian chief was dead—killed by a final rifle shot—and about half the band of seventy-five had been killed.

It was the assigned duty of the volunteers to reconnoiter to determine the approach of Mexican armies and bands of hostile Indians and to give the alarm to the militia in case of a full-scale invasion. Any smaller difficulties they were expected to handle themselves. For this they were to furnish their own arms, equipment, and horses—at least at first. In theory the government provided their ammunition and supplies; but in practice they usually lived off whatever game they could shoot, and frequently their commander paid for their ammunition himself. They were promised $30 a month pay; at first none of this was forthcoming; but later, as the government's credit improved, they were paid. Their commander received $75 a month; later this was increased to $150. At times there were as many as 500 men in the field from the various companies. But it was a dangerous life, and few survived: it was said that about half of them were killed every year.

If one thing was remarkable about Hays's leadership of the Rangers, it was his ability to deal with opponents far superior to his strength in numbers. He was never defeated, and seldom was he fought to a stalemate. In 1842 Hays's Rangers emerged triumphant from the Battle of Painted Rock in present Llano County, in which the odds against them were greater than in any other of their many battles. In it forty Rangers overcame about six hundred Comanches. It began while Hays was absent from San Antonio on a patrol with two small companies; while he was gone, the Comanches raided near the city. On his return, Hays prepared to go after them. Riding 130 miles in 42 hours, he led his men ahead of the fleeing Indians. Then he halted and waited. The Rangers camped on the north shore of a small lake about 100 yards wide and 300 yards long, which would be approached only from its north shore. On its south rim rose Painted Rock, 100 feet above the water.

Tired from their long ride and expecting to camp several days and recuperate from their hardships, the Indians advanced toward the lake to refresh themselves and their mounts. Their surprise was complete when the Rangers opened fire on them. Withdrawing in haste, the Indians returned and examined the incoming trail made by the Rangers as they had approached. From their examination the Indians were able to determine that the Rangers were very few in number; they planned, therefore, to rush and overwhelm the small force at daybreak.

The Rangers, meanwhile, took up a position in a thicket of willow trees on the shore, thus screening and protecting both themselves and their horses from flying arrows. At daybreak the Indian attack came; throughout the day the Indians charged their position. Each time they were driven back. In the evening they retired, but small parties harassed the Rangers throughout the night. Desperately thirsty after their long ride, the Indians sent a party twenty miles for water.

The next day the battle was renewed. Now the Indians opened a new front from the top of Painted Rock, but their arrows were not effective at that range. The Rangers' bullets were. That night the Indians again made their twenty-mile trip for water. On the third day they attacked again.

Now the Rangers noticed a chief who seemed to assume a leadership position among the Indians. Wearing buffalo horns as his headdress and carrying a heavy buffalo-hide shield, he had thus far proven impervious to the bullets of the Rangers. Many fired at him, but none could penetrate his defense. It was this chief who assembled the Comanches for a final massive and concerted assault—one that very probably would have succeeded. But, as he turned to rally his men, he turned his shield also, exposing for a minute his side. The minute was all that was needed. In an instant Hays had felled him. Seeing their fallen leader, the Indians rushed to recover his body, but Ranger fire drove them back. At that point a Ranger mounted his horse, rode out, lassoed the body, and dragged it back to the Ranger position. Furious, the Indians charged again. Once more they were driven back, and this time, deprived of the leadership of their chief, they left for good. The Rangers, meanwhile, discovered that the Indians' *caballo* had been left behind the lines, their guards unaware that the battle had been abandoned. These they seized, killing the four guards left with them.

Hays wanted to rest his men and horses, but his food and ammunition were exhausted, so instead the party returned immediately to the camp on the Medina. Over one hundred Comanches lay dead on the battlefield, and many more had been carried off or died later of their wounds. The Rangers had one man wounded and one horse killed. This was a typical result of their encounters—rarely did they suffer severe casualties.

Only once did Hays lead his men into an ambush; that was at the Battle of Bandera Pass. In September or October, 1841, Hays and a company were camped about seven miles west of San Antonio on Leon Creek. Breaking camp to scout for Indians, they marched northwest up the Medina River, camping overnight on the present site of Bandera. The next day they marched toward Bandera Pass, about ten miles away. Meanwhile, a large band of Comanches heading for the Medina Valley reached the pass before the Rangers did, discovered their approach, and laid an ambush for them.

The Apache Indians had been decisively defeated by General Bandera of the Spanish army at the same place about a hundred years before; from him the pass derived its name. Hays reached the southern end of the pass about 11 a.m. and started to ride through it, suspecting nothing. The pass was approximately 500 yards long and 125 yards wide; its sides were steep slopes, 50 to 75 feet high and covered with brush and large boulders, behind which the Indians were concealed.

Waiting until the Rangers were securely inside the pass, the Indians opened fire with arrows and bullets. Disorganized by the suddenness of fire and the plunging of their terrified horses, the Rangers temporarily lost control of themselves. The Indians then charged but did not come within hand-to-hand combat range. Struggling to hold their horses and at the same time fire effectively, the Rangers were almost routed by the onslaught, until they heard Hays's voice. Their reaction to his instructions was a demonstration of their ultimate faith in his judgment and ability. "Steady there, boys. Dismount and tie those horses; we can whip them—no doubt about that." And they believed it, coming from him; at once they calmed and rallied to the necessities of their situation. Soon they had collected themselves and were firing with good effect. The Indians charged repeatedly, with many hand-to-hand encounters, for about an hour before they decided that further engagements were useless and retreated to the end of the pass where they had tied their horses. Five Rangers had been killed in the encounter and five wounded, along with many horses.

Probably no single action of Hays did more to establish his reputation as an Indian fighter than his lone fight at Enchanted Rock in Gillespie County. In the fall of 1841 Hays was one of a party of fifteen or twenty men employed to survey some lands near Enchanted Rock. This formation derives its name from an Indian legend that for many years a few warriors had used this rock as a fort, defending themselves against hostile tribes until they were finally killed. From that time it was held in awe and reverence by Indians who considered the rock the home of these warriors and performed religious rites on its summit, perhaps offering human sacrifices. Enchanted Rock is a huge mass of solid granite, covering about 640 acres and standing between 400 and 500 feet above the surrounding country. Its top is fairly flat, covering about two or three acres, and with a few shallow depressions.

At the time of his engagement Hays and a party of about twenty men were locating and surveying land near the head of the Pedernales River. Though there was a large Indian camp in the vicinity, Hays strayed from the group, as he often did; or perhaps he left specifically to inspect the fabled rock. He soon was jumped by three Indians, who were shortly joined by five or six more. At about the same time that Hays was attacked, his party was set upon by another group of Indians. Hays moved toward his men, halting frequently to exchange shots with his pursuers. When his horse began to tire and the Indians started gaining, he made for Enchanted Rock.

Hays dismounted and scrambled to the top of the rock. The Indians knew who he was and were anxious for his scalp as a prize. He kept them off by threatening them with his rifle (for they knew his prowess with it); finally he killed an Indian, threw his rifle aside, and opened up with his precious new five-shooters. He drove them back several times, but more arrived from their camp. After an hour about one hundred Indians surrounded him and prepared a massive assault. Just before they attacked, his surveyors arrived—having defeated the Indians attacking them—and drove off his attackers. At the end of the engagement there were five or six dead Indians lying on the ground around Hays's position, and more lay around the base of the rock.

Hays's promotion to major in 1841 was said to have come to him as a result of his fight at Canon de Ugalde. Early in June, 1841, Hays and a detachment of sixteen Rangers and twenty Mexicans under Captain Flores were scouting for Indians, toward the Canon de Ugalde On June 10, as they were nearing the Canon, they saw Indian signs. Hays left his men to reconnoiter; he discovered there were twelve Indians in the camp and that they were evidently scouts three or four miles in advance of the main body. Hays mounted his horse and crossed the creek before them, exposing himself at sixty or eighty yards.

A hundred yards from the camp was a dogwood thicket in the center of which were three ash trees and a big log on the ground. The Indians broke and ran for the thicket; immediately, one was killed by a shot from a Ranger's gun. The Rangers dismounted, tied their horses, and surrounded the Indians. Hays and two other Rangers, one named Trueheart, entered the thicket, which was extremely thick. The Indians fired, wounding Trueheart in the neck and Hays in the finger and killing the third man. Hays carried Trueheart out and reentered alone, with a double-barreled shotgun and a pistol. He crawled through brush till he was close to the Indians. Three, armed with bows and arrows, charged him, but it was impossible to shoot arrows accurately in the brush. Hays waited for the charging Indians. When they were within fifteen steps of him, he fired both barrels of his shotgun, killing an Indian with each. He then drew his pistol on the third man, who ran. Hays left the thicket, got a Yeager rifle, and reentered. He fought for nearly three hours, killing all but one of the Indians. This last fellow had a gun, making him more deadly than his companions. He concealed himself behind a log. Hays, just a few feet away, could just see the top of his head. Finally both fired at the same instant. The Indian's bullet grazed Hays's shoulder; Hays killed the Indian. The Rangers, fearing pursuit by the main body of Indians, collected the Indians' horses, improvised a litter for Trueheart, and left immediately for camp near San Antonio.

Escapades with marauding Indians were not the only exploits in which Hays won his reputation in arms. When General Adrian Woll invaded Texas in 1842, Hays was in San Antonio. Exercising that natural leadership which seemed to come to him in an emergency, he quickly organized about 175 San Antonio citizens into companies. After Woll entered the city, Hays escaped, rode to Seguin, and spread the alarm; he then returned to draw the invaders out of San Antonio. He and his followers battled them outside the city, but Woll soon withdrew again to safety in its buildings. The Texans attempted to pursue Woll when he returned toward the Mexican border, but internal dissension among the men prevented any effective action against him.

The failure to carry out an effective pursuit of Woll led to an outcry for an invasion of Mexico by the Texans. Although President Houston generally favored a defensive rather than an offensive policy against the Indians and Mexicans, in October, 1842, he ordered Brigadier General Alexander Somervell to take command of Texas troops and to be prepared to cross the Mexican border. Houston gave Somervell broad discretionary powers, and there was no official action when he organized his forces in the still largely Mexican town of San Antonio instead of in the more eastern settlements as had been expected. Hays played a role, though not a major one, in the ill-fated Somervell Expedition. When the expedition disbanded, at least two of the men in his company—Samuel H.

Walker and "Bigfoot" Wallace—volunteered to go with Fisher on the Mier Expedition.

When Somervell was sent to take command of the Texas troops, Houston advised him to take advantage of Hays's talents and "to obtain his services and cooperation." Hays offered his services to lead a spy company. This brought about almost immediate dissension because a spy company commanded by Captain Samuel A. Bogart had been promised that it could remain intact with Bogart at its head. In the end a compromise was arrived at by which Bogart would be in command when Hays was away from camp and Hays would command in Bogart's absence.

The expedition finally set out from San Antonio on November 25, 1842. The weather was cold and rainy and the men short of provisions. When the Nueces was reached, the stream was so swollen that Hays advised constructing a crude bridge over which the remainder of the force could cross. Hays reached Laredo on December 5, and after some scouting decided that no large Mexican force was in or near Laredo. While on the scouting expedition, Hays captured two Mexicans, one of whom was injured by the Indians when captured. The prisoner escaped, presumably to go back to Laredo.

For days the force existed in a state of indecision. On December 11, Somervell paraded the men and announced that all who wanted to go home could do so. Two hundred of the seven hundred men left for home. Then he moved his force across the river to a hillside near Guerrero on the Mexican side of the Rio Grande. From there he sent Hays into the village to obtain horses. Hays was told that the horses had been driven into the interior upon the approach of the invaders. Somervell then sent Hays to demand that the *alcalde* give the force five thousand dollars or the town would be sacked. When the *alcalde* told Hays that only a few hundred dollars could be collected, Somervell backed down and decided to order the force to abandon the operation.

Before he turned back, however, Somervell gave permission to William S. Fisher to lead an expedition into the interior. There is some disagreement as to Hays's activities at this point. Some say that he remained behind for a few days to perform scouting duties for the group that became known as the Mier Expedition. Others say he stayed behind to search for a fine horse that he had lost. In any case, by January, 1843, Hays was back in San Antonio with plans for an effective defense of the southwestern frontier.

The Mexican War, too, saw Hays and his Rangers in action. Some time before Congress declared war on Mexico, General Zachary Taylor at Fort Brown had called on Texas for 5,000 volunteers—two regiments of infantry and two of cavalry. A small company of ex-Rangers was scouting for him before the Battles of Palo Alto and Resaca de la Palma and had participated in these two battles. Hays was elected to command the First Regiment of Texas Mounted Volunteers. Its nucleus was formed by Hays's Rangers; and although they were regularly enrolled volunteers, the public and press always referred to them as "Texas Rangers."

Hays's force left Matamoros on August 9, 1846, planning to work itself across the countryside on a mule-buying expedition made possible by the presence of a mounted regiment. By October he had reached Monterrey, and it was said that 200 of the 450 men who attacked Independence Hill there were Texas Rangers.

Hays's Rangers were notable for three things—their effectiveness in battle, the terror they inspired in the civilians in the territory they captured, and their colorful dress. To many of the Texans the war was an opportunity to avenge the treatment that they and their fellow Texans had suffered at the hands of the Mexicans. Long experienced in fighting the Mexican bandits who ventured north into Texas, some of the men apparently felt that they had merely changed their bases of operations rather than their foes.

While other soldiers were dressed in regulation military attire, the Rangers kept the garments they had worn on the frontier. Instead of uniforms they wore an odd assortment of clothes, usually including red or blue shirts, and a wide variety of hats. They furnished their own horses and apparently most of their arms. Each was armed with a short rifle or shotgun, one or two holster pistols and Colt revolvers, and a Bowie knife. A contemporary observer notes, "The Rangers made it a point to look as ferocious as possible; practically all of them, with the exception of Colonel Hays, wore long beards and mustaches." Although the Rangers did not complain about the lack of uniforms, they did object to the lack of tents. Their shelters were made of whatever brush they could find in the vicinity of the places where they camped.

The invaded country viewed them with awe and terror, not alone from their reputation as "a sort of semi-civilized half man, half devil, with a slight mixture of lion and snapping turtle, and [had] a more holy horror of them than . . . of the evil saint himself." An eyewitness to their progress into captured towns observed, "They rode, some sideways, some upright, some by the reverse flank, some faced to the rear, some on horses, some on asses, some on mustangs, some on mules. On they came, rag, tag, and bobtail, pell-mell, helter-skelter, the head of one covered with a clouched hat, that of another with a towering cocked hat, a third bare-headed, while twenty others had caps made of the skins of every variety of wild and tame beasts; the dog, the cat, the bear, the coon, the wildcat, and many others had for this purpose all fallen sacrifice, and each cap had a tail hanging to it, and the very tail too, I am keen to swear that belonged to the original owner of the hide."

The Rangers' reputation as fighters was confirmed in the campaign at Monterrey. Indeed one veteran wrote, "I was with the regulars but . . . had it not been for their [Hays's and McCulloch's] unerring rifles, there is no doubt we would have been whipped at Monterrey." Nonetheless, the Mexican War damaged the Rangers' reputation. The men were no longer in Texas, where infractions of civilized law such as assuming the role of judge, jury, and executioner, as well as lawman, were tolerated if the victim were a Mexican or an Indian who could be presumed to be guilty.

The lack of discipline showed itself badly. General Taylor, who came to dislike the Rangers intensely, said he could not stop the pilfering of the Texans: "I have not the power to remedy it. . . . I fear they are a lawless set." He further remarked that they would be the best soldiers in the volunteers, "but I fear they are and will continue [to be] too licentious to do much good."

After Hays returned to San Antonio from Monterrey, he requested permission to organize another regiment of volunteers. This request was finally granted in March, 1847, after Hays visited Washington in an effort to have the recruiting regulations changed so that men could be enlisted for short terms. The second unit was also called the First Texas Mounted Volunteers (3rd Service) and was organized during April and May. While in San Antonio, Hays interrupted his recruiting long enough to marry Susan Calvert but apparently did not let domestic life interfere with military duties.

At about the same time that Hays was in Washington, changes were made in tactics of the war. President James Polk ordered Winfield Scott, highest-ranking general in the army, to Vera Cruz. From there he was to move to Mexico City. Scott's most serious problem was that he could not keep his lines of communication open. In September, apparently at the express command of President Polk, Hays was ordered to take his force to Vera Cruz and then proceed to Mexico City. His mission was to clear the road of guerrillas.

Hays's force left Vera Cruz on November 2 en route with General "Jo" Lane's brigade to Puebla. Their first duty there was to rescue twenty-one Americans who were being held by the Mexicans at Izucar de Matamoros. Not only were the Americans freed, but also enough horses and ammunition were captured to equip them. Late in the month Hays and his men moved on to Mexico City. From that time they were sent out on a variety of expeditions against guerrillas in the vicinity. One of these expeditions was to Tehuacan on January 21, 1848. Santa Anna was reported to be there with about a hundred cavalrymen and the inevitable guerrillas. Before they reached the place, the troops met a coach, which was protected by a safe-conduct pass. Over the protests of Hays, who maintained that the men would take news of their arrival to Santa Anna, the coach was allowed to pass. The next morning when the force arrived at Tehuacan, Santa Anna's apartments were deserted; the cloth still laid for a meal and burning candles were testimony to the general's rapid departure.

The Texans did, however, have an opportunity to see Santa Anna before both they and he left the country. The Rangers were camped near Jalapa when news came that Santa Anna, his daughter, and his wife would pass nearby. John S. Ford was there and said he thought "the old warrior's face blanched a little at the sight of his enemies of long standing."

With the end of the Mexican War the Texans returned home. Having annexed the state, the United States government also took over the problems of waging war on the Mexicans and the Indians who threatened the frontiers. Zachary Taylor was elected President in 1848, and he had no love for the Texans and the tactics they used to terrorize guerrillas. From the beginning the Mexican War had been an unpopular one in parts of the country where it was condemned as a war to extend slave territory. And, as the war progressed, more public condemnation was heaped on the Rangers' tactics than upon the guerrilla activities that inspired them. Although other factors affected the election, results of popular opinion were reflected in the victory of the Whigs and Zachary Taylor over the Democratic candidate Winfield Scott.

Almost as soon as his service in the Rangers ended, Hays was involved in a different kind of adventure on the frontier. In 1848 the businessmen of San Antonio wanted to establish trade with El Paso, Chihuahua, and other points west. This valuable trade had been going to Missouri, and they wished to divert it to themselves. Since the intervening areas were unexplored, a route suitable for wagons was not known. The businessmen agreed, therefore, with government aid, to support an exploring expedition. The government hoped to learn the best route along which to station troops on the frontier. Hays was chosen to lead the "Chihuahua-El Paso Pioneer Expedition." His party consisted of seventy-two men: thirty-five citizens from San Antonio, Fredericksburg, and other cities; thirty-five Texas Rangers; and two guides and interpreters. The purpose of the expedition was to mark out and open a good wagon road between San Antonio and Chihuahua.

The expedition left San Antonio August 27, 1848, carrying thirty days' rations and one pack mule for each four men. Hays struck north for a Ranger camp on the Llano near Castell, where he was to meet a military escort. At the Ranger camp he was joined by Captain Sam Highsmith and thirty-five Rangers. The combined forces left early in September, reaching the Pecos on September 26, 1848.

Until they reached the Pecos, all went well: game was plentiful, water was frequently found, and the weather was good. But west of that stream, no one, including the guides, knew the territory, and the expedition got lost. The food gave out; water became scarce. Occasionally they were lucky; once they came across four old buffalo bulls which provided them a supply of meat; but this too, was finally exhausted. Samuel Maverick, one of the well-known persons who accompanied Hays on the trip, wrote in his account of the venture that by the sixth of October they were "eating mustang meat."

By the time they reached the banks of the Rio Grande, the supply situation had not improved. They killed a panther and ate it; they ate grass; finally they killed and ate two pack mules. At last they crossed the river into Mexico; on October 17 they camped near the Mexican village of San Carlos, then turned up the river to Presidio del Norte. Finding that their strength was nearly exhausted, they made their way to Ben Leaton's fort, where they ate and rested for sixteen days; additional help came from the Bishop of Chihuahua who visited them and furnished them animals and supplies. But winter was coming, and even with the additional supplies the men were still poorly provisioned. They thus decided not to try for Chihuahua but to turn toward home. They split into three parties: twenty-eight men were to march directly to San Antonio; Hays and six men went southwest to Las Moras Creek; Highsmith went northwest to the Concho. Highsmith's Rangers were caught in a severe thunderstorm at the head of Brady Creek and suffered from their poor clothing. Although they reached San Antonio before Hays's party, Highsmith died soon after their arrival. Hays's men met with the same kind of obstacles that had haunted their trip west; but they struggled to within eighty miles of San Antonio, where they met a detachment of United States troops who gave them food. They reached San Antonio December 11, 1848.

As a result of his expedition, Hays reported that the best route for a wagon road was from San Antonio north to the San Saba and thence through the Concho country to the Pecos.

By this time Hays apparently was doing well financially. Early in 1849 he erected a fine stone residence at Buena Vista, opposite Mier, Mexico, on the Rio Grande. There he formed a partnership with Captain Jack Everett to conduct a general merchandise and commission business. They erected a large warehouse and operated a ferryboat; probably it was abandoned or sold, for the same year Hays left for California.

In 1848 President James K. Polk offered Hays an appointment as commissioner of Indian affairs for the newly-acquired Gila River country. Hays accepted and found that his first duty would be to start from San Antonio and contact the tribes on the Gila for the purpose of establishing a treaty with them. In 1849 Hays received his appointment and started from San Antonio. Accompanied by Major John Caperton, with whom he was to be closely associated in years to come, he left the Alamo City with forty men once more to make his way to El Paso. He camped opposite old El Paso nearly five weeks and succeeded in making contact with the Indians; but the Apaches were not disposed to make a treaty, and he decided to go to Tucson. There a man in his caravan became ill, and Hays and eight others stayed with him. When the sick man had recovered, they left Tucson with one wagon and reached San Diego almost starved. From San Diego Hays took the brig *Frémont* for San Francisco. He also submitted his resignation as Indian commissioner.

In California Hays was to acquire great wealth and property, as well to achieve notable political and social stature. It is ironic that though he had given so much to Texas, he should have to find his fortune elsewhere.

When Hays arrived in San Francisco, he found an election underway for county officers and entered the race for sheriff. His chief opponent was furnishing food and drink (no doubt leaning more toward generosity in the latter) for the voters. Hays chose to earn the voters' faith by a display of horsemanship on the public streets. Riding a hot-blooded and spirited animal, Hays charged onto the scene of the voting and proceeded to put his mount through a spectacular display of pirouettes and caprioles, so impressing the populace that they immediately elected him their man. It was April, 1849, and the first county election held in San Francisco.

In 1850 Mrs. Hays joined her husband in California. After her arrival he moved outside of town, but by the end of 1851 he had returned because the office of sheriff was demanding all of his time. Fernwood, the home he ultimately built for his family, was just outside Oakland. The 800-acre site had a large supply of underground water and boasted hundreds of trees and shrubs, with extensive lawns and gardens and graveled walks. Here he reared his two children, John C. and Elizabeth. Four other children died in infancy.

Hays evidently was a popular sheriff and quite efficient by the standards of the day. Apparently he brought some of his attitudes toward lawbreakers with him from his service in the Texas Rangers. He maintained, for example, "cordial relations" with the San Francisco vigilantes, who were very active, and even enlisted their support in providing a better jail. Once he evidently succeeded in seizing a prisoner from them, only to have them retake him and hang him. These disagreements, however, were apparently infrequent.

During his tenure as sheriff Hays also engaged in a practice which today would be less than applauded. The California Legislature leased state prisoners for ten years to two contractors, who agreed to guard and maintain the convicts in exchange for their labor; Sheriff Hays and his deputy Caperton subleased the contract and used the prisoners to work in a rock quarry on Angel Island and to cut and grade the San Francisco streets. The practice continued about four months, but Hays lost money on it and terminated it.

In 1853 Hays attended Franklin Pierce's inauguration to attempt to secure an appointment as federal surveyor general for California. This office had been created by Congress in 1851, and Hays would be the second man appointed to the position. He took a four months' leave of absence from his job as sheriff and with his friend Major Richard P. Hammond visited the capital city. Both he and Hammond were already acquainted with Pierce, and apparently this assured Hays's receiving the position.

After Pierce's inauguration Hays did not return directly to California but went to New Orleans and then to Texas, visiting old friends. Four days after returning to California, he resigned as sheriff.

He held the position of surveyor general of California until 1858, when he was appointed to the same post in Utah Territory, where the previous officeholder had resigned. Prior to this there had been much speculation that President Buchanan would not reappoint Hays surveyor general of California. There seems to have been some touch of scandal connected with his holding the position, for in a letter he wrote to the President thanking him for the new appointment, he mentioned that he was grateful for its helping to clear his name. In February, 1859, Hays resigned his appointment as surveyor general of Utah because he did not wish to move his family there. During the period of his commission he neither went to Utah nor received any salary for the job.

Apparently fulfilling his duties as sheriff and surveyor general did not restrict Hays's business activities, for he became a wealthy man. In 1852 he became interested in land on which present Oakland stands. At the time it was owned under a Spanish grant by Vicente Peralte, who was having a difficult time maintaining it against squatters. Hays and certain other citizens relieved him of this tribulation by purchasing the land from him. In this way, Hays became one of the founders of present-day Oakland.

Hays became both a social and economic force in the San Francisco area—and indeed in all of California—and was involved in many of the most important affairs of the state. In 1858 he played a leading role in trying to move the state capital to Oakland. The state was at the time paying thirty thousand dollars a year rent for housing the legislature, supreme court, and charity institutions. Hays's name headed a list of eight Oakland men who bound themselves to guarantee this expense until suitable buildings were constructed and to give twenty acres of city land to be chosen by the state as a site for the buildings, as well as to provide "a temporary state house" and to construct certain other buildings for which Hays put up collateral of $20,000. The legislature, however, voted down the proposal. In 1869 Hays made a contract with the University of California regents to locate that institution's agricultural college lands.

His prosperity increased continually. In 1877 he was assessed $162,700 for local property taxes. His and Caperton's land along the waterfront was valued at an average $3,000 per acre. During the last years of his life, his estate was estimated at over half a million dollars— he was offered $300,000 for his waterfront land in Oakland alone. His ranch at Oakland in 1875 was located on the present site of the University of California, and he owned both waterfront property and city lots in San Francisco. In addition to being a major stockholder in the Oakland Gas, Light, and Heat Company, he was a founder and director of the Union National Bank and of the Union Savings Bank, and he owned a number of ranches throughout the state.

Hays was also prominent in Democratic politics in later life. He was a delegate to nearly every state convention, and as a delegate to the national convention at St. Louis in 1876, he placed in nomination the name of Samuel J. Tilden.

Perhaps the most tumultuous event occurring during Hays's time in California was the Civil War. Hays maintained a neutral stance during the conflict, though he was offered the rank of general in both the Union and Confederate armies. In March, 1861, he was appointed brigade inspector in the state militia by Governor John G. Downey, indication of the trust which both factions had in him.

It was while he was living in California that Hays had his last Indian fight. This took place, however, not in California but in Nevada. In 1860 Virginia City was a mining town where many Texans, Californians, and others had gathered. Against these intruders the Piute Indians went on the warpath. Among their depredations perhaps best known is the massacre of Major Ormsby and forty-six men sent to punish them for a raid on a stage station. There are two versions of the story of how Hays became involved in this episode. One tells that there was an old Texas Ranger, Captain Edward Storey, a man of great courage and very popular among the people, working at this time in the mines of Virginia City. Captain Storey at once raised a company—the Virginia City Rifles—and proceeded against the Indians. Hays, hearing of the efforts of his old comrade in arms, came from California with several companies to help him. The second version is that Hays arrived on personal business at Carson Valley, Nevada, just as the Indians began their war. The citizens then asked Hays to take charge of a volunteer regiment, and Hays accepted their draft. Plagued with too many volunteers and free-loaders and a lack of sufficient horses, guns, and rations, Hays nonetheless succeeded in driving the Indians back into their mountain retreat and chastening them sufficiently so that an army troop stationed there afterwards was able to contain them. After ten days' service, he disbanded his volunteers.

After the 1870's Hays was living a semi-retired life on his ranch as a stockman and capitalist; in the spring of 1878 he was reported to be retired and did not maintain an office in town. Nevertheless during the 1870's and early 1880's he served as a director of the state institution of education for the deaf, dumb, and blind. In December, 1879, he went to Arizona to seek relief from his rheumatism and to investigate a prospective business venture for his son. In January of the following year, he became seriously ill, but by the end of the next month he appeared to be improving. Apparently he realized his last days were drawing near, for he began about this time assigning his property to his wife and son, retaining only a little over $10,000 worth of property in his own name.

Hays died at the age of sixty-six at his ranch near Oakland on April 21, 1883. His family wished a simple funeral from his home, but the citizens of that city demanded an opportunity to pay their respects to him. The result was a "partial military funeral" and the most elaborate Oakland had ever seen.

Thus ended with an appreciate tribute the life of the man who had formed the organization and the image of the Texas Rangers. More than that of any man who followed him, Hays's character determined the nature of the organization he did so much to establish. Today, the code by which the Rangers fought seems harsh and inhumane. To indict Hays for his adherence to this code makes it possible to lose sight of the essential quality of this man—mild in appearance and demeanor and yet as tough and self-reliant as the conditions under which he lived demanded.

Samuel H. Walker

Samuel Walker's charge into Huamantla, Mexico -- October 9, 1847

Samuel H. Walker

by

JAMES M. DAY

His friends all said that Samuel Hamilton Walker was endowed with unquestionable bravery, natural leadership ability, and a "quiet kindly manner." Such were the qualities that endeared him to his Ranger comrades and made him an example of the corps. Whenever Rangers of the Republic of Texas period are mentioned Walker's name is invariably included alongside those of John C. Hays, Ben McCulloch, and Richard Addison Gillespie as the four who set the standards Rangers have followed for over a century. Walker's Ranger service lasted not quite five years, but that was enough for both McCulloch and Hays to pronounce him as "one of the best spies or rangers on this continent." Both men agreed that Walker was superb at "prying out the designs of the enemy," and that for such tasks they both preferred Walker "to any other man living."

To say that Walker rode in the shadow of Hays, McCulloch and Gillespie would be misleading; instead he rode manly by their side and on occasion emerged as the leader. That seemed to be Walker's sole passion—to lead Rangers in killing Indians and Mexicans, both of whom were the enemies of his beloved Republic of Texas. As a Ranger leader he was successful; however, his everlasting fame has come from the fact that he assisted, perhaps directed, Samuel Colt in developing the Walker Colt revolving pistol, a superior weapon used in both the Mexican War and the American Civil War.

Thus, Samuel H. Walker, member of Jack Hays' famed Indian campaigns of the early 1840's, soldier in the Mier Expedition of 1842, captain of dragoons in the Mexican War of 1846, and designer of a significant weapon of war, earned a niche in American frontier history. His life span extended a mere thirty-two years, his Ranger service not quite five; yet, he undoubtedly counted his life a success because he fulfilled his ambition, emerged a Ranger leader and died leading Walker's Rangers in battle.

Walker's date of birth is recorded on his tombstone in San Antonio as being 1815. His place of birth was Prince George County, Maryland, and *Niles National Register* of Baltimore proudly claimed him as a native son. His parents, Nathan and Elizabeth Walker, produced a family of seven: Johnathan, Nathan, Charles, Jane, Catherine, Mary, and Samuel. In addition, Sam Walker had one half-sister, Elizabeth, and a half-brother, Henry. When the Ranger died, he had not married so the members of his family were his only heirs. Little of his childhood is known, but his letters reflect that he had good command of the English language and that his expression was as forceful as his actions. He appears to have had a fundamental education.

Walker's military career began in May, 1836, in Washington, D. C., his home since 1832. Seminole Indians under Osceola had massacred over one hundred soldiers under command of Major Francis L. Dade, and volunteers were being sought in Washington to retaliate. The battle scene was in far-off Florida, but Walker was not daunted by the distance or the danger. He enlisted and served for two years, making two trips to the swamp land and emerging as a corporal. His promotion came as a result of the "exceptional courage" he displayed in a battle near Hacheeluskie in January, 1837. Thereafter, Walker was used often as a guide and scout, training which later contributed substantially to his Ranger activities.

By October 9, 1837, Walker's Washington City Volunteer Company was back at home to be mustered out; however, their service was not ended. Additional troubles caused their return to Florida, and they were in St. Petersburg by December 8. It was a short trip, though, and by February 20, 1838, the company was in Charleston, South Carolina, en route to Washington. They arrived home in March.

In Florida, Walker had made a friend of Lieutenant George Gordon Meade, an officer charged with erecting Fort Foster some twenty miles from Tampa. Walker was guarding the engineer's operations when the two met in 1836, but the following year Meade quit the engineers to supervise construction of the Alabama, Florida, and Georgia Railway. When Walker was released from the army in 1838, he returned to Florida to work on the railroad, and he remained there until the end of 1841 when he took the trail to Texas, his land of destiny.

John Caperton, one of John C. Hays' original Rangers, noted in his memoirs that Walker arrived in San Antonio in January, 1842, over one year after Hays had organized his ranging company. Bigfoot Wallace recalled that Walker was not one of the first rangers, but that he soon joined. Caperton noted that Walker's first service was with an expedition organized against Indians who had massacred a family and had taken two children as captives. The force recovered the children, but Walker's role in the action was not recorded.

Since the muster rolls of Hays' Rangers were destroyed by fire, and since Walker appears not to have distinguished himself enough to warrant mention, his presence with Hays' men at the Battle of Calaveras Creek and at the Battle of Bandera Pass in 1842 is mere speculation. Bigfoot Wallace noted the capture and execution of horse thieves around San Antonio in "1840-1841." On one occasion a notorious thief named Antonio Corao was ordered executed by Hays, and Wallace, Chapman Woolfolk, William Powell, and Sam Walker were the four who dispatched Corao. Wallace was recalling the event long afterwards, so his dates might have been confused.

San Antonio existed in a charged atmosphere in 1842 as the Anglo-Americans attempted to maintain what they had gained up to that point. Enemies present were the Indians, mostly Comanche, and the Mexicans who were still smarting from the independence the Texans had won at San Jacinto. Since the territory between the Nueces and the Rio Grande was in dispute, its environs furnish the scenes for some of the bloodiest combat Texas has ever witnessed. Twice that year Mexican forces took San Antonio as Indians constantly lurked nearby ready to kill the aggressive white man.

A Mexican army estimated at from five hundred to seven hundred men headed by Raphael Vasquez occupied San Antonio on March 5, 1842. After two days of plundering and negotiating, the force retreated to the Rio Grande, but the resentment left in the wake was an item of significance. During the summer the Texas Congress was called into special session to pass legislation demanding an offensive war against Mexico. President Sam Houston vetoed the measure, but Adrian Woll's September capture of San Antonio caused him to relent as he ordered the formation of an army of invasion. Houston placed Alexander Somervell at the head of the army and appears to have given Somervell two sets of orders —one calling for invasoin of Mexico and and war, and the other cautioning restraint.

Adrian Woll, a Frenchman at the head of a Mexican army of almost one thousand men, approached San Antonio on September 10, 1842. During the night of the 10th and morning of the 11th, Woll's forces surrounded the city and invested it. Like Vasquez, Woll held the town for ten days before returning to the Rio Grande with the prisoners he selected. Unlike Vasquez, however, Woll met with limited armed resistance from the Texans who by this time were comparable to a hive of swarming bees.

Into this hive of activity rode Sam Walker as a scout for Captain Jesse Billingsley's Company of Mounted Volunteers. Billingsley's Company was from Bastrop, and they arrived in the Texan camp on the evening of September 18. The Texans were not numerous as they had only about 350 men, but among the group were their strongest leaders. Matthew (Old Paint) Caldwell was the commander, while the scouting company was commanded by John C. Hays, ably assisted by Henry E. McCulloch. Billingsley's force of one hundred, aiming to join Caldwell's motley group, had placed Walker and Crockett Peerey out front as spies. In the course of their explorations, the two men came upon the scene of the famed Dawson Massacre shortly after it happened. It must have been an electrifying sight to observe the dead bodies of thirty-five men, enough to sicken even a hardened veteran. After Walker and Peerey dutifully reported their observation, the decision was made to avoid the scene in order to find Caldwell. Woll's forces were simply too numerous for an open encounter. John Henry Brown, an eyewitness to the events, noted that Walker was "on his first campaign in Texas."

As Woll evacuated San Antonio, he drew in his wake a group of Texans who did not want to let him escape to the Rio Grande. Those men were the Rangers of Hays, and among them was Walker. Hays had a brief encounter with Woll's rear guard on the morning of September 22, but the ground was so boggy from heavy rain that Caldwell's troops could not reinforce the Rangers. Woll made good his retreat to Mexico, a journey of ten days.

The Texans then repaired to San Antonio to begin organizing the Somervell Expedition. Not until two months later did the Texans, a force of only 750 men, leave San Antonio. On November 13, 1842, they began their trek to Laredo. After a delay at the Medina River, the men arrived at the Nueces River on December 2, and made an approach to Laredo on December 8. The companies of Hays and Captain Sam Bogart traveled together in order to act as spies for the main body, and their trip was uneventful—except for the weather. Rain accompanied by a norther caused both horses and men to wear themselves out in the mire. Hervey Adams, a member of Bogart's command, noted in his diary that the norther was "about as cold a one as I have seen in Texas." The weather worked a wonderful equality on the men, while the horses suffered so much that some were left for their bones to bleach in the earth. Finally the army left the bogs and by the time the Nueces was reached the men were in fine spirits, ready to forget the natural enemy, weather, to get at their mortal enemy, the Mexican.

They infested Laredo peaceably enough, moved down the Rio Grande to make a requisition for supplies on the town of Guerrero, before the commander Alexander Somervell, decided to order the troops to retreat to Gonzales. The date was December 19; the Texans numbered 498 men. Of that number only 189 actually returned with Somervell, while the remainder organized themselves into new units led by William S. Fisher. The split was quite dramatic as Hays allowed his men to decide individually which way they would go. Two of his men, Sam Walker and Bigfoot Wallace, pleaded for Hays to lead the way, but he would not do so. Instead, Hays remained with Fisher's men only a few days to act as a spy as they progressed down river. Walker was among Hays' men who crossed the Rio Grande, entered Mier, and returned to warn Fisher of the large force the Mexicans were collecting there. Early on the morning of the 24th Hays left camp to return to San Antonio, but he did so only after warning his friends to abandon the invasion. Neither Walker nor Wallace would listen, but their subsequent experiences caused them to gain increased respect for the wisdom of their Ranger commander.

Ranger service had led Sam Walker this far, and he was not about to back up. He took on an enlistment as a private in Ewen Cameron's Company A. As such he was assigned to Lieutenant John R. Baker's detachment of spies, an organization formed in the best tradition of the Rangers. These twenty-five men were placed on the Mexican side of the Rio Grande as the force advanced toward Mier. On December 23, Fisher's men marched unopposed into Mier, demanded supplies, and then returned to Texas soil. By the morning of the 25th, Christmas day, Baker's spies reported that almost 700 Mexican soldiers had entered Mier. Here was a force worthy of the Texans' attention, a challenge to rise to and conquer; they determined to attack. Their move began at 2 p.m. and the Rio Grande was crossed in two hours. Just as they were starting the march to Mier, Baker sent word to Fisher that two of his most efficient spies, Samuel H. Walker and Patrick Lusk, had been captured.

Ingloriously, Walker did not participate in the Battle of Mier. While his capture was a serious matter, it has to have a speck of the comical in it. As a spy he was in the vanguard to do battle. In attempting to get a shot at the enemy, Walker mounted a fence that led straight to the Mexicans. He fired his shot, then tried to make his escape by crawling through the fence. A big Mexican seized his boot and held it so tight that Walker could not extract his foot. Other Mexicans came to help until finally the big soldier overpowered the slender Walker, pinning the Ranger to the ground. If the scene had ludicrous aspects to it, its result was deadly serious—Walker was a prisoner of the enemy he so wanted to destroy; he was the first to be taken prisoner at Mier.

Bigfoot Wallace, another of Baker's spies, later gave an account of Walker's confrontation with the Mexican General Pedro Ampudia. According to Wallace, Walker was not "afraid to speak his piece." Threatening Walker's life, Ampudia ordered the Ranger to report the numbers and intentions of the Texans. The Ranger replied coolly that Fisher's command numbered only three hundred. Ampudia was surprised that so few men would attack his large army on his own ground, and Walker is said to have stated confidently that the Texans would pursue and attack the Mexicans even into hell. Other than that Walker remained silent and would not be used in any way. When Ampudia came to offer terms for the Texans to surrender, he used Dr. J. J. Sinnicksen as the message bearer.

The Texans did in fact march into Mier, fight their battle, and surrender. By 4 p.m. on December 26, 248 of them were captives of the very troops they had sought to destroy. Even though Ranger Sam Walker was reunited with his comrades, his future could not appear bright. Certainly they could expect no kindness from their captors. On the roll of prisoners compiled at Mier, Walker was listed simply as a carpenter. Mockingly, the force was marched under guard down the Rio Grande through Camargo to Matamoros. Humiliatingly, the Mexicans held a grand parade as the proud *Tejanos* passed through each community. From Matamoros, Walker and his companions were marched to Monterrey and Saltillo. Depressed, weary, and hungry, the force left Saltillo on February 7, 1843, headed south to San Luis Potosi. Their guard consisted of three hundred soldiers of the famed "Red Caps" commanded by Colonel Manuel R. Barragan.

By the evening of February 10, they had marched 120 miles from Saltillo to arrive at a small place named Rancho Salado. The time had arrived for an attempt to escape, an effort the Texans later referred to as "The Battle of the Rescue." Unquestionably such an aggressive force as the brash Texans would be difficult to hold. The Mexicans knew that and thus assigned crack troops to the guarding task. Even before Salado the Texans had twice planned escape attempts, but they had an informer in their midst so they cancelled the attempt each time. Now, however, at Salado, the time was ripe. In typical American frontier fashion, the prisoners exercised their voting rights to elect their commander. The mantle fell to the Scotsman, Ewen Cameron, commander of Walker's Company A.

At sunrise on February 11, Cameron gave the word for storming the guard. As the Red Caps were drawing their morning rations, the Texans observed that most of the Mexican muskets were stacked against a wall about ten paces from their door. At that moment when all was calm, that one instant which military commanders try to train against, Ewen Cameron, sensing instinctively the rightness of the time, yelled the signal for freedom. In a voice which rang through the entire ranch, Cameron ordered the attack. Sam Walker had supported the attempt from the beginning because, as Wallace put it, Walker "was bitter about the whole thing." When Cameron issued the order to move, Walker was by his side. Some observers say that Cameron and Walker went into the courtyard side by side, and others report that Cameron was first and Walker second. The sequence is inconsequential because the result was that desired—the Texans, with five killed, made a complete success of the escape. They overpowered their guard and then headed toward Texas.

Once on the trail northward they made a serious, almost fatal, blunder. Instead of keeping to the main road which probably would have allowed them to get to Texas, they turned into the mountains hoping to avoid capture. There they became thirsty, hungry, and exhausted, and were recaptured and returned to Saltillo. Looking akin to "a congregation of the newly-risen dead," Sam Walker and 133 other Texans marched under guard into Saltillo on March 1, 1843. There President Antonio Lopez de Santa Anna ordered them all to be executed, but the Mexican governor, Francisco Mexia, refused to obey. After three weeks at Saltillo, the aggregate of 176 Texans were placed under a new guard to resume the trip to San Luis Potosi. By March 25, they walked into Rancho Salado once again along with an ill-omened whirlwind. The time had come for them to pay for their daring escape.

The Texans were lined up to hear the edict of Santa Anna, words which dropped on them like thunderbolt from the sky. In a daze they heard that one in ten must die immediately by the firing squad. The famous "Lottery of Death" or "Black Bean" incident was at hand, and Samuel H. Walker had to participate. Into an earthen jar were placed 159 white beans and seventeen black ones. They were shaken well as each Texan had to draw for his life. Ewen Cameron drew first and got a white bean. Walker, when his turn came, likewise drew white; but seventeen of their comrades drew death and were shot. The next morning the living Texans marched out of Rancho Salado and from the road they could see the "stiffened and unsepulchered" bodies of their dead comrades. Many a Texan vowed revenge that day against the Mexican nation; Walker died later in an attempt to attain that vengeance. Their sufferings were in no way over as Ewen Cameron was summarily shot on April 25, and Walker found that he had another score to settle with the Mexicans.

Still, Walker's humiliation was not ended. The Texans were taken to Santiago prison where they were given new clothes. Afterward, they moved to the prison at Powder Mill near Tacubaya where they had to build a portion of a road leading to Santa Anna's palace. They were at the Powder Mill on July 4th when they celebrated "the birthday of the land of the immortal *Washington*." With Judge Patrick Usher presiding and Israel Canfield acting as secretary of the meeting, F. M. Gibson made an appropriate address before the appointment was made of a committee to draft a preamble and some proper resolutions. Samuel H. Walker was on the committee along with Thomas W. Murray, William Ryon, William H. Van Horn, J. G. W. Reirson, and William McMath. The resolution reflected the pride of the prisoners by stating that they had "unshackled hearts" and that they were unsubdued in spirit. They claimed pride in Texas by denouncing Sam Houston for his fight with Commodore E. W. Moore and stating that Texas should vigorously prosecute the war "she is now engaged in." They thanked all the persons who had shown them kindness, then sent the resolutions to the editor of the New Orleans *Picayune* for publication. On September 12, 1843, the Texans left Tacubaya headed for the well-known Castle of Perote, but Walker was not among the group. His fateful acquaintance with the castle had to wait about four years, and it would take place under entirely different circumstances.

Perhaps the July 4th celebration set him off, for without doubt, Walker was one of the most arrogant of the Texan prisoners, who as a group were lazy and sullen. Undoubtedly, Walker on occasion provoked the Mexican guards with the sharpness of his tongue. A story told by William S. Oury reflects such an attitude. Oury was not a Mier man, but he later knew Walker as a Ranger. They rode together, and around the campfire at night Walker told stories to Oury, who included some of them in his reminiscences many years later. One day while Walker was working on Santa Anna's road at Tacubaya, a guard struck Walker on the back with a whip. The Ranger's temper was such that he "sprang upon the offender with the fury and strength of a tiger." He had many scores to settle, but other guards were present and they came to the rescue of their comrade. Walker was subdued, so severely hurt that he was sent to the hospital. The expectation was that he would die, but he did not. On July 30, Walker, James Charles Wilson (an Englishman), and D. H. Gattis made good their escape.

They started on the way to Tampico where they planned to catch a ship to the United States. Between Tacubaya and Tampico they were retaken four times, but by one ruse or another were able to reach the seaport. The first time they were captured, the three were able to bribe the officials for the price of one dollar per head, a total of three dollars. When Tampico was reached, Wilson took passage to New York while Walker boarded the schooner *Richard St. John* bound for New Orleans. He was no doubt a pleased man as he set foot on United States soil in late September, 1843. Walker had many memories, but he definitely had not forgotten his promises of vengeance against the Mexicans—vows which soon caused his fellow warriors to call him "Mad" Walker. The Mier expedition had not at all tamed this Texas Ranger.

At maturity, Walker was not an imposing looking person. His height was about five feet, ten inches, and the adjectives "slender" and "spare" are invariably applied to his make-up. He had reddish hair, usually wore a small beard which was red, and his eyes were a mild blue color. Walker often was described as having a slouchy appearance even though his manner was gentlemanly. Scarce with his words, he was not at all on the extroverted side. As the two men became good friends, some observers noticed that Walker even took on some of the habits and manner of expression of his Ranger captain, John C. Hays.

Such was the man who spent little time in the Crescent City in 1843. Instead, he booked passage to Galveston and by the end of the year was in San Antonio ready once more to become one of Jack Hays' Texas Rangers. The year 1844 gave Walker opportunity to prove that he was one of the best.

Hays' Rangers had a busy time in 1844 and 1845, mostly with Indians. Equipped with a single-shot rifle or a double-barrelled shotgun, a knife and a hatchet, and two of Samuel Colt's famous five-shooter pistols, the Rangers rode up and down the South Texas frontier punishing the marauding Indians wherever contact was made. Early in the spring, Hays took fifteen men, including Sam Walker, on a sortie on the frontier. They rode for three uneventful weeks before deciding to return to San Antonio. When they came to Sister Creek near its confluence with the Guadalupe River, a scout discovered a bee tree. Two Rangers were in process of robbing the tree when twenty-five Indians were discovered. As Hays led his men in a charge, two other lines of braves were discovered sitting on top of an adjacent hill. Both groups were ready for battle, so Hays' men retired to timber as the Indians attacked using arrows and spears, verbally issuing war whoops in an effort to frighten the Rangers. As the Rangers approached the trees, an unseen group of Indians from within let forth a volley of arrows. Undaunted, the Rangers reached the brush, dismounted and proceeded to the defense. Time after time the Indians circled the grove hurling arrows and spears at the occupants, and repeatedly Ranger rifles and pistols answered the challenge until the Indians finally withdrew to a rise in the prairie for a council.

At that moment the Rangers took the initiative and attacked. A shower of arrows injured three of the Texans, but comrades held each one in the saddle as Hays and his men broke through the Indian line and charged back again. Prudently the Rangers returned to the brush in an effort to protect the wounded. Just as the trees were reached Walker shot an Indian who was trying to thrust a spear into the Ranger. At that moment, when Walker's back was turned, another warrior drove a lance through him. Ranger John Carolin shot the Indian while William S. Oury helped Walker to the thicket. Then, after Richard Addison Gillespie was wounded by an arrow, the Comanche war chief closed in to finish the kill. Gillespie, wounded but calm, sent a bullet into the chief's head as the Rangers en masse reached cover. The Indians recovered the body of their leader, and carrying their wounded and dead, began a retreat. Hays, with only seven men behind him, followed the Indians until darkness forced him to return to the grove to attend the eight wounded Rangers, one of whom was Walker.

None of the Rangers died, but upon their return to San Antonio, Walker had to convalesce for several months. As a result, he was unable to participate in the reorganization of the Rangers who were ready for action by March 15, 1843. Hays had been authorized forty privates and he no doubt saved a slot for the courageous Sam Walker. Walker probably watched the rodeo in San Antonio which featured some of Buffalo Hump's Comanche braves, Mexican rancheros, and Hays' Rangers, but his infirmity prevented his participation. He likewise missed a battle with the Comanches in the Nueces Canyon in April, 1844; however, by May he was ready to ride again.

This time Hays had fourteen men with him as they camped on Walker's Creek at a point about equidistant from Austin, Gonzales, and San Antonio. Over seventy-five Comanche Indians led by Yellow Wolf were discovered, and another battle was on. The opposing forces used several ruses, but neither attacked full scale. Finally the Indians withdrew to a brush-covered height and began to shout insulting phrases in Spanish at the Rangers. Methodically, although somewhat angry from the insults, the Rangers skirted the hill to attack from the rear. The surprise worked as the Texans formed a V-shaped wedge and caught the Indians still looking for them at the front. The Comanches turned in an effort to drive the white men off the hill, but the Rangers retaliated by forming a circle of defense. Then the Texans turned from their rifles to their Colt revolvers and proceeded to inflict heavy punishment upon their foe. In the second Indian attack, Walker was lanced several times and so was Ad Gillespie, but twenty-one Indians lay dead and several others were wounded. Only thirty-five braves were able to answer Yellow Wolf's call for a third attack. Ad Gillespie, though wounded, was able to shoot Yellow Wolf, after which the Indians withdrew from the scene. Twenty-three Indians were found dead and at least thirty more were seriously wounded, while the Rangers lost one man and had four wounded, Walker among them.

Hays attributed the victory to the Colt revolving pistols, weapons which proved so deadly that the Rangers fired not over 150 shots. This was the battle scene that Sam Walker later immortalized in a sketch he drew to be engraved on the Walker Colt pistol. After the battle the wounded Rangers were moved to San Antonio for recovery, and Walker was among those left under the care of Mrs. William B. Jacques.

Walker recovered satisfactorily and continued in the Ranger service, even though the pay was neither high nor steady. Early in 1846 he petitioned the legislature of Texas for financial relief to the amount of $230. Thirty dollars was for his board and attendance in the summer of 1844 while he was sick and wounded. This apparently was as a result of the battle at Walker's Creek. In the same battle, Walker lost his horse, a mare valued at $100, while rescuing two of his "wounded companions who were in a perilous situation." The other horse, also a mare, was valued at $100 and was lost in an Indian fight in the spring of 1845. Walker explained his plight: "For this kindness and attention I believe no earthly reward or compensation from me was anticipated nor will any charge ever be made, which places me under a two fold obligation to see that a just compensation is made." He further explained that the pay to the Rangers was "rather insufficient to meet actual necessary expenses, and that he relied on the justice of the government for money to pay an indebtedness he had incurred in their service. John C. Hays certified the truth of Walker's statements, but the legislature did not honor the petition.

The horse lost in the spring of 1845 was probably killed near Corpus Christi in a battle with a renegade Cherokee. The skirmish was in a Ranger battle with a small party of Comanches. Walker singled out the Cherokee, a fugitive, because the latter was showing such bravery and skill in battle. Several shots at close quarters were fired with the result that the Cherokee's horse was killed and Walker's was wounded. Walker was thrown to the ground and as he rose, he was hit in the shoulder with an arrow. Colt's five-shooter made the difference that day because Walker had one bullet left and he used it to relieve the Cherokee of life.

Such wounds as Walker received caused his fellow Rangers to nickname him "Unlucky Walker." His courage was such that he invariably was in the thick of the fight, and because of that he seldom came away from a battle unscarred. If his courage endeared Walker to the Ranger leaders—Hays, McCulloch, Gillespie—his endurance and performance of duty were added bonuses. Ranger William Oury told the story of a scouting expedition which met with such obstacles that the members wanted to return to camp. They were out of supplies, their goal was miles away, the trail was made difficult by rain, and some Rangers who were to rendezvous with the group failed to appear. The party was so disheartened that they proposed to call off the scout; all, that is, except Sam Walker. He simply stated that he would follow his orders to go, alone if necessary, to the place designated. Walker's determination won, the group went forth, and, as Oury stated the facts, "after great suffering from toil, exposure, and hunger, accomplished their mission." Such grit was what made Sam Walker a leader of Texas Rangers.

As the days passed in 1844 and 1845, the need for defense of the Texas frontier did not lessen. The Rangers did become such a potent force that their leader, Hays, was sometimes able to negotiate with the Indians rather than fight them; however, the Comanche still continued their depredations and the Mexicans became more antagonistic. Hays broke his force into three platoons so they could cover more territory. One of the platoons was led by Hays, one by Ben McCulloch, and one by Ad Gillespie. Late in 1845 the force was reorganized into a battalion of three companies. Walker, on September 28, 1845, enlisted for a six-month term in the unit commanded by his long-time comrade, Ad Gillespie. In the election for a lieutenant of the company, Edward Ratcliffe defeated Walker; however, rank was a fleeing object to the Rangers for Captain Gillespie later served under Lieutenant-Colonel Sam Walker, and Lieutenant Ratcliffe lost his life on May 8, 1846, while First Sergeant of the spy company commanded by Walker. Walker rode the South Texas brush country with Gillespie until his six-months term passed. At San Antonio on March 28, 1846, Sam Walker was honorably discharged as a private from the "Texas Mounted Rangers." He took with him the physical scars of many an Indian battle—those he had proudly earned—and the internal scars of his captivity in Mexico for which he did not yet have revenge. Walker, at age thirty-one, was ready to make the Mexicans pay.

His opportunity came as the United States, in annexing Texas, came into conflict with Mexico. A full six months before President Anson Jones issued his proclamation on the demise of the Republic of Texas,

General Zachary Taylor, the "Old Rough and Ready" of the Florida wars of the late 1830's, had a force of United States troops at Corpus Christi. Their location at the mouth of the Nueces River was significant because all land south of there was claimed by Mexico. The land dispute was one reason the soldiers were present. Taylor's army remained at Corpus Christi until late March, 1846, when he stationed himself in the semi-tropics near present Brownsville. With both Americans and Mexicans anticipating trouble, the fighting was not long in coming. Taylor and his men were new to South Texas; they needed scouts to show them the secrets of the Rio Grande. Sam Walker made himself available.

He had visited Austin and Washington-on-the-Brazos with Hays in late March and April, 1846. Their purpose was to talk with Governor J. Pinckney Henderson about raising a regiment of Texas Rangers to assist Taylor's army. At Brenham the people appropriately welcomed the two Rangers. They were taken to a grove where a leading citizen, John Wilkins, Sr., made an address praising the Rangers. Afterward, a barbeque was held, and that evening there was "a gay ball." The next day the two Rangers headed eastward to raise recruits, but they heard that the Mexicans were threatening Taylor's communications. At that time, Walker went to join Taylor and Hays returned to San Antonio.

Walker had several things to recommend him to such a man as Taylor. One point in common was that they had been in the Florida Seminole Wars together, although General Taylor probably did not know Corporal Walker. But Lieutenant George Gordon Meade, who had known Walker in Florida, had joined Taylor's ranks at Corpus Christi in August, 1845. Perhaps Meade was the one who recommended Walker to Taylor. Another possibility was that Walker, as a member of Gillespie's company, had made himself so conspicuous that Taylor recognized his worth.

When Taylor and Walker conversed on April 16, 1846, the outcome was beneficial to both. Taylor authorized Walker to recruit a company of "Texas Mounted Rangers" to act as scouts for Taylor's growing army. Walker had friends in the area—men who had a grudge against all Mexicans, and from them he chose the "most fearless dare-devil spirits." From the Mier expedition came John Brannan, J. J. Humphries, Gideon K. Lewis, James Neely, and George Washington Trahern, while his Ranger experience brought Edward Ratcliffe and Creed Taylor. Walker's company was mustered into service on April 21 for a three-month period, and it had the same status as Hays' ranging companies. These men were Texas Rangers in the Federal service. Ninety-three Rangers served in the unit during its brief existence, before the final muster on July 16, 1846.

Using his position to fullest advantage Captain Walker rapidly became a national hero, epitomizing all that is brave and intelligent in the American people. He more than any other man in those first critical days of the Mexican War established the standard of what a leader should be; he did it Texas Ranger style—by leading instead of pushing. The American nation later responded generously to his deeds.

Fort Texas, begun early in April, was designed to serve as an outpost to observe the movements of Mexican forces under Generals Mariano Arista and Pedro Ampudia. It was on the north side of the Rio Grande across from Matamoros. Major Jacob Brown commanded the fort, which was about four miles from Taylor's headquarters. Taylor needed to keep the communication line open so he chose Walker's Rangers for the job. Walker's camp was in the open, about midway between Point Isabel and Taylor's main force.

The vicinity was infested with Mexicans who were raiding the American supply trains. Walker learned of a raid on the night of April 28 and he set out to locate the robbers. Leaving fifteen men in camp with orders to be on the alert, Walker rode boldly toward the Arroyo Colorado, but the action that night was at the home camp instead of with Walker. A large troop of Mexican cavalry attacked the camp, killing all but two men, G. W. Trahern and Morris Simon. Twelve Colt pistols, four carbines, and three North's rifles were among the equipment lost to the Mexicans. Such a loss of men and equipment would undoubtedly have stained Walker's reputation had he quit then. Instead, the outrage spurred him to bravery.

The attack showed that the Mexicans were closing in. Walker, feeling that he had to warn Taylor of the danger, called for volunteers to ride Ranger style through the Mexican lines to warn the general. With six Rangers, he achieved the goal. When Ampudia's troops crossed the Rio Grande at the end of April, Taylor was ready because he had been warned by Walker. The event gained for Walker a fair amount of praise which helped offset the sting of two days earlier.

The next problem cropped up at Fort Texas, or Fort Brown as it came to be called. Mexican artillery opened fire on the fort on the morning of May 3. Major Brown reported the action, but Taylor was worried. He needed more information, and he called on Walker's Rangers to get it. Taking three Rangers and Captain Charles May, Walker set out to penetrate Mexican lines to talk with Major Brown. May was to rendezvous with Walker that night but when Walker failed to appear, May returned to headquarters on the morning of May 4. Walker's supposed death "cast a gloom over the whole army," reported one participant, because the Ranger was "a general favorite." Gloom turned to cheer the following morning as Walker returned alone. He had lost his horse, but reported to Taylor that Brown could hold as long as he had food and supplies. The press corps generously advertised Walker's actions so much that he became a national hero overnight. One Ranger historian noted that Walker's heroics near Fort Brown "set an example for other Texas Rangers to emulate; and it spread the name of the Texas Ranger for the first time beyond the limits of Texas." Those who described a Ranger as "a dirty shirt and five-shooter" were beginning to see something important.

When Taylor's army set out on May 7 to relieve Fort Brown, Walker's Rangers were in front acting as spies. The day was excessively hot as Walker's scouts methodically weaved back and forth through the brush, ever sensitive to the movements of the enemy. They made contact shortly after noon, and the Battle of Palo Alto was fought then and there. Walker and his company gave good account of themselves before the Mexican force withdrew about sundown.

The following morning, Arista's Mexican army started southward; Taylor waited a while and then followed. At about four in the afternoon the American advance party, a group which included Walker's Rangers, began flushing small Mexican units. This formed the signal for the two forces to meet at Resaca de la Palma, and again the Americans were victorious. With the battles over for a while, Taylor's forces rested while the United States Congress voted a declaration of war.

Walker's separate service was temporarily ended, but it was not forgotten. The populace of New Orleans raised some money, purchased a horse named Tornado, and sent the animal to Walker by means of the steamer *Alabama*. It was a "magnificent horse" presented to Walker "for his courage and perseverance in effecting a communication with Fort Brown during its bombardment, and while it was surrounded by the enemy." One man who scrutinized the events in late May wrote from Matamoros: "Captain Walker (I believe now a major) is here with his men. He rode by our quarters yesterday on *Tornado*, the horse sent here from New Orleans to him. Tornado seems as fond of his backer as the backer does of him, and they were the observed of all observers. Walker's men say he has but one fault and that is too brave for his discretion."

As the war expanded and more troops were needed, additional Texas Rangers were demanded. Two mounted regiments which were formed were commanded by Colonels John C. Hays and George T. Wood. As fate decreed, unlucky, mad Sam Walker was once again, but for the last time, to serve with his Ranger *compañero*, Hays. The First Regiment

Texas Mounted Rifles straggled into Taylor's from May to July; Hays himself arrived on May 22, 1846. Eventually Walker's company was absorbed into the regiment, and Walker himself became the lieutenant-colonel, second in command. Taylor's need for spies provided a task the Rangers took to with alacrity.

Creed Taylor made the statement that "Walker's scouts were allowed precious little time to engage in the frivolities of garrison life." They were sent to Camargo and even to Mier, the spot where Walker had been captured four years earlier. One day eleven Rangers led by Walker were scouting near the pueblo of Chupa on the San Juan River when they spotted a troop of soldiers bathing in the water. They decided to attack and since the Rangers were dressed as Mexicans, they were able to get quite close before being identified. By the time the captain asked if they were "Tejanos," it was too late because Walker's Colt revolver had fired; the captain was dead. Ranger bullets killed the other Mexicans as they bathed in the stream, and it was like hitting ducks at a shooting gallery. The hail of lead was so effective that not over five Mexicans escaped. After burning the Mexicans' possessions, the Rangers intently moved on.

Their next exploit was to capture a herd of eight hundred cattle intended for Ampudia's army. As the Rangers approached the herd, the question was raised as to what eleven men would do with so many cattle. Some discussion took place until Walker easily settled the matter. They would capture the herd for Taylor's troopers. Walker captured the drovers, and he had an interesting torture treatment scheduled for them. Their boots were removed and each one was tied to a horse. As the horse moved through the brush, the cactus, mesquite, and other thorny plants literally sliced the riders' feet to shreds. Walker was getting some revenge; he had walked that same route as a Mier prisoner. Then the herd was rounded up and started for Camargo. They drove all night but were overtaken the next day by five hundred Mexican cavalrymen. The Rangers abandoned the cattle as Walker sent to Hays for assistance. Only Walker, John Himes Livergood, and Creed Taylor watched the Mexican force move the herd southward again. In the moonlight that night the three men saw two riders heading south. Then, as they hid, Walker "at a glance" recognized Hays. After the two Rangers conferred, the Texans attacked the Mexicans, took the cattle, and safely drove them to Camargo.

On June 24, 1846, Sam Walker became the lieutenant-colonel of Hays' regiment, a reward he had earned by his daring and had attained by election. Six days later he accepted appointment as a Captain, Mounted Rifleman, in the United States Army, but he was permitted to stay with the Rangers until they were mustered out on October 2. At that time Walker reverted to his captaincy, the rank he held the following year when he was killed.

Lieutenant-Colonel Walker gave good service to his Ranger comrades and to Taylor's army. As the Americans moved toward Monterrey, the Rangers acted as the antenna of Taylor's force. Creed Taylor noted that they were so far out front that they saw precious little of the Americans until Monterrey was reached. Then, in late September, Hays' Rangers led General W. J. Worth's soldiers up the incline of Independence Hill to take the Bishop's Palace. It was a hard-fought battle with Hays leading one column and Walker the other. On this spot Walker lost a dear friend, one with whom he later shared his grave, as Captain Richard Addison Gillespie fell in the thick of the fight. After Independence Hill, the Rangers led Worth's troops into Monterrey. and again they were in two columns, one led by Hays, the other by Sam Walker. Inch by inch they worked their way toward the main plaza; Hays was on Calle de Monterrey and Walker was assigned the heavily barricaded Iturbide Street. Methodically the two thin lines of Rangers stretched their cords toward the heart of the city. They won the battle, the city surrendered, and on the last day of September, Taylor started mustering out the Rangers. Walker ceased to be a lieutenant-colonel on October 2. It was the highest rank he ever held as a Ranger, but was not necessarily the peak of his career. He seemed to be at his best as a captain, when he had his own command and was able to operate with independence and initiative. This man was an individualist of the first order.

Presumably, Walker remained at Monterrey for two weeks after his discharge until Hays had completed his official reports. Then the two Rangers rode to San Antonio. From there they went to Houston where they boarded the steamer *Sabine* for Galveston. They arrived in Galveston on the morning of November 5th to be greeted by a lengthy eulogy in the Galveston *Civilian*. The article stated that the two Rangers were "distinguished before and since the beginning of the war between the United States and Mexico." They were "in the morning of life" at a time "when honors most elate men," but, the editor noted, "they wear their laurels as modestly as if unconscious of their existence." Galveston leaders entertained the fighters with a fine dinner and a ball.

Afterward Walker and Hays sailed for New Orleans only to find that news of their destination had preceded them; their arrival "created a sensation throughout the city." They became "lions . . . as they walked through the streets." Thousands greeted them and were charmed by the fact that "such brave hearts" were found in men "so unpretending in appearance and so totally free from assumption of manner or thought." New Orleans wanted to celebrate their visit, but Hays had to hurry to Mississippi and Walker had urgent business in Washington.

The urgency was connected with his military appointment as Walker had to recruit his company of mounted riflemen, train them, and head to Mexico to force death to visit some more Mexicans. This visit to the east absorbed almost six months of Walker's short life; still it proved fruitful because Walker and Samuel Colt met and developed the Walker Colt pistol. It was a signal achievement for both men and a boon to the United States Army. By mid-November Walker was at Washington, and he was in New York by November 30, in contact with Sam Colt. Walker and the Rangers had used Colt's five-shooters since 1838 and they had found them to be most effective. More than once Colts machinery had saved Ranger lives, Walker's included. Some stories reflect that Walker and Colt met as early as 1840, but such tales are founded on rumor. Walker did not arrive in Texas until 1842, Colt went broke in 1841, and the Rangers were still using the Paterson Colt five-shooter up until the Mexican War in 1846. Between 1841 and 1846, Colt lived in penury, existing mainly on his dreams. He had heard of the exploits of the Texas Rangers with pistols and he was anxious to hear the reports from those who had actually performed such feats. Colt, on November 27, 1846, took the initiative when he heard that Walker was in New York attempting to buy weapons.

Colt wrote to Walker:

> Dear Sir:
>
> I have so often herd you spoaken of by gentlemen from Texas that I feel sufficiently acquainted to trouble you with a few inquires regarding your experience in the use of my repeating Firearms and your opinion as to their adaptation to the Militatry Service in the War against Mexico—I have heard so much of Colonel Hayse and your exployets with the Armes of my invention that I have long desired to know you personally & get from you a true narrative of the vareous instances where my arms have proved of more than ordinary utility—
>
> Such is the prijudice of old officers in our Armey against aney invasions upon old & well known impliments of Warfare that as yet I have not been able to introduce my arms in the servis to an extant that has proved proffitable, But I am in hopes of getting an action this winter in there favor if I am not disapointed in the recommendations I may be able to collect to submit to congress.
>
> I hope you will favor me with a minute detail of all oc-

casions where you have used & seen my arms used with a success which could not have been realized with arms of ordinary construction. Let me know at where a letter will reach Col. Hase. I wrote to him some time since at Monteray but presume he did not receive my letter—

Should Col Hase take the command of the regiment ordered from Texas & desire them armed with repeaters I have but little doubt but that his requisitions would be complied with at once

It has also occurred to me that if you think sufficiently well of my arms to earge the President & Secy of War to allow your company to be thus armed you can get them the arms are very much Improved since we first commenced there manufacture & I have no doubt that with the hints which I may get from you & others having experience in there use in the field that they can be made the most complete thing in the world—

The letter elated Walker so much that he penned an immediate reply:

New York City Nov 30th 1846

Mr. Saml Colt

Sir—

In compliance with your request I take great pleasure in giving you my opinion of your revolving patent arms.

The pistols which you made for the Texas Navy have been in use by the Rangers for three years, and I can say with confidence that it is the only good improvement that I have seen. The Texans who have learned their value by practical experience, their confidence in them is unbounded, so much so that they are willing to engage four times their number. In the summer of 1844 Col J C Hays with 15 men fought about 80 Comanche Indians, boldly attacking them upon their own ground, killing and wounding about half their number. Up to this time these daring Indians had always supposed themselves superior to us, man to man, on horse—at that time they were threatening a descent upon our Frontier Settlements—the result of this engagement was such as to intimidate them and enable us to treat with them. Several other Skirmishes have been equally satisfactory, and I can safely say that you deserve a large share of the credit for our success. Without your Pistols we would not have had the confidence to have undertaken such daring adventures. Was it necessary I could give you many instances of the most satisfactory results. With improvements I think they can be rendered the most perfect weapon in the World for light mounted troops which is the only efficient troops that can be placed upon our extensive Frontier to keep the various warlike tribes of Indians & marauding Mexicans in subjection. The people throughout Texas are anxious to procure your pistols & I doubt not you would find sale for a large number at this time

          Yours very respy
         S H Walker Capt Mounted
           Riflemen U S A

By the time of their meeting, they were friends. Walker could brag about Colt's pistols, and Colt thought he could supply arms for Walker's men. They toured the New York gun shops looking for pistols, but not a single Paterson Colt was for sale. When Walker stated that perhaps it was just as well because the Paterson Colt had some defects, Colt demanded to know them. Methodically the somewhat embarrassed Ranger spelled out the failings to the inventor. They retired to Colt's room to a conversation which lasted long into the night, but when it ended Colt had the ideas for a new weapon. Moreover, Colt knew that Walker's prestige and position could get him back into the pistol business. That night the two Sams made an agreement: Colt was to modify his weapon and Walker was to press the government to purchase them.

When Walker returned to Washington, he made an appointment with President James K. Polk. Together the two men went to the office of the Secretary of War, William S. Marcy, where Marcy was instructed to make the purchase. That same day, Lieutenant Colonel George Talcott, the Ordnance chief, was commanded to place the order. He did so with reluctance because he had long been opposed to Colt and his new invention. Talcott did comply, and Colt had his order for one thousand pistols to cost $25 each and to be delivered in three months. Walker personally was to supervise the purchase.

Walker had done his work so thoroughly that Colt was left with a problem. He had an agreement, but no factory and no machinery; he did not even have a model of his old pistol. Colt knew that Eli Whitney had a foundry with the capability of producing the new pistol, but Whitney, when approached, refused to consider a contract because he had more orders than could be handled. Colt was stymied there, but he turned to his old friend Orison Blunt to make a model of the Paterson pistol so Colt and Walker would have something concrete to talk about. The model was finished by early January, 1847, when Walker returned to New York. The United States government had given Walker authority to negotiate the contract with Colt, so he was there for that purpose.

Walker saw the model and approved it after some modification, so the contract was signed on January 4. It provided:

> Memorandum of an agreement made this 4th day of January 1847 between Samuel Colt (inventor of Colt's Patent Repeating Pistols) and Samuel H. Walker, Capt. U. S. Rifles, and acting by authority of and direction of the Secretary of War, for the immediate construction of 1000 or a larger number if hereafter determined by the Secretary of War, of said Colts patent Repeating Pistols, made to correspond with the model recently got up by said Colt and Walker and being as follows, viz,
>
> The barrels to be nine inches long and Rifles made of the best hammered Cast Steel and of a bore suited to carrying round balls, fifty to the pound with strength sufficient to firing an elongated ball weighing Thirty-two to the pound.
>
> The cylinders to be made of hammered cast steel with chambers for six charges each, and of a length, size, and strength, sufficient to be charged with an elongated ball 32 to the pound.
>
> The lockwork with the exception of the hammer to be made of the best cast or double sheet steel and the parts sufficiently uniform to be interchanged, with slight or no refitting.
>
> The Hammer and lockframe to be of the best Gun iron and case hardened.
>
> The stock to be of sound black walnut, bound and secured by a strong strop of iron.
>
> The Pistols answering to the above specification *to be maid* with the least possible delay, and to be paid for at the rate of $25 each on delivery,—in New York in passels or lots of 100 each. The first hundred of said arms to be completed, if possible, in three months from the date this contract is confirmed by the Secretary of War, and all the remainder as soon thereafter as possible, and not under any circumstances to exceed five or six months if the arms can possibly be completed by the dividing up of the work or the employing of two sets of hands to work night and day.
>
> In addition to the arms, it is agreed between the parties that there shall be furnished one entire set of springs for every 10 pistols, one entire lockwork, one spring vice extra set of cones and screws for every 25 pistols One Bullet mould for every 10 Pistols to cast one elongated ball. *One do* to every 50 Pistols to cast six elongated balls at one casting.

One Powder Flask, one screw driver, one nipple wrench, and one lever for driving home the balls for each pair of Pistol. For the whole including the additional sixth chamber in the cylinder and all the above mentioned extra fixinngs, a price, not exceeding *Three* to be allowed on each Pistol in addition to the Contract price.

The above contract subject to the approval of the Secy of War.

        Saml Colt
        S H Walker Capt
         Mted Riflemen
          U S Army

Colt went to work with such vigor that he persuaded Whitney to undertake the actual manufacture of the pistols at the same time he and Walker were working out minor changes. Then Colt subcontracted from Whitney the pieces of the pistol which he, Colt, could produce. The contract called for production in three months, but in spite of all of Colt's efforts the weapons were not completed until July 6. On June 26, 1847, Captain William A. Thornton completed the inspection of 220 of the pistols which were immediately shipped to Walker at Vera Cruz.

This weapon has variously been referred to as the Whitneyville Walker Colt, the Model of 1847 Army Pistol, the USMR Pistol, and simply the Walker Colt; however, Samuel Colt gave it perhaps its most appropriate name. He invariably referred to it as "Walker's pistol," a fitting tribute to the man who showed him how to make it and in turn pushed the order to him. That the two men worked together with utmost harmony is revealed by the engraving Colt placed on the cylinder of later versions of the weapon. During February, Colt urged Walker to draw a western scene commemorating the Texas Ranger victory over Yellow Wolf. Walker somewhat reluctantly complied by drawing a sketch showing Jack Hays on a white horse and Walker on a black horse. It is a scene of action as the Rangers are chasing Indians. Colt used the drawing for an engraving which was stamped on the cylinders of the pistols. This was Walker's only claim to fame as an artist.

While Colt was manufacturing the weapons, Walker returned to Washington where he lobbied in the Congress for Colt's interest. He could do only a limited amount of this because he was after all an army officer. Undoubtedly the Texas congressmen and senators backed Colt, and Walker was able to get support from some others. Also, Walker was able to get the strength of his company increased from seventy-six men to 110 men, and each soldier in Walker's Company C was to carry two of Colt's pistols. Walker spent most of January and February in recruiting duty at Fort McHenry near Baltimore, but, as early as February 19 he knew he was scheduled to report to New Port Barracks, Kentucky. He wrote this to Colt and asked him to hurry the pistols. By March 19, Walker was at the post on the Ohio River training his men. He begged Colt for results as he wrote:

> Newport Barracks Ky
> March 19th 1847
>
> Dear Colt
>
> My hopes are all on the[e] my dear fellow and I trust I shall hear something from you in a few days that will be interesting, do for heavens Sake rush things as rapidly as possible and send me some of the Pistolls immediately I want to commence drilling my men on horseback with them I have now 120 men with me and will enlist 180 more to take out with me, everything now is depending on you, let me hear from you immediately if not sooner and let me know when they will be forthcoming, find out how things are likely to work in relation to inspection &c and let me know all about it, Could you not get Mr Whitney to turn all his force upon them and turn them out immediately if you will only manage to get them turned off rapidly and forward me enough to arm my detachment before leaving, "you shall wear the brightest Laurel of our first victory and the Glory shall all be thine," yours in hast
>
> S H Walker
> Capt M. R.
> Rcetg Officer

In April, 1847, Walker's training at New Port Barracks came to an end. His men were needed in Mexico. Company C, United States Mounted Rifles, left Kentucky for New Orleans, where they caught a steamer bound for Vera Cruz. They docked on May 10. When they joined General Winfield Scott's command the men were "in good order and ready to mount." As one observer expressed it, Walker's men "were very acceptable to the Americans at the moment." Walker himself brought his personal servant, a slave named David who was to care for the captain. The Walker family had insisted on this, but the Ranger noted later that his servant was of little value. The troop of dragoons remained near Vera Cruz for almost a month before they were stationed at Perote Castle, the place where Walker's comrades on the Mier Expedition had been imprisoned. Perote Castle in the mountains of Mexico was Sam

Walker's last home; it was a brief but explosive stay of approximately four months.

Walker, first with Scott as he had been first with Taylor, was assigned the task of keeping open the National Road between Vera Cruz and Jalapa. As the supply trains of the American army lumbered over the mountain expanses, they invariably were attacked by Mexican guerrillas. Sam Walker, using the guerrilla tactics of the Texas Rangers, kept the road as safe as possible under the circumstances. J. J. Oswandel was present as Walker's men rode into Perote "mounted on fine spirited horses." The soldiers were "all fine, strong, healthy and good looking men," and "nearly every one measured over six feet." Walker no doubt had learned how to look tall in the saddle! Oswandel concluded: "So *robadores* (robbers), take warning . . . for the renowned Capt. Samuel H. Walker takes no prisoners."

Throughout the summer Walker remained at Perote feeding the guerrillas a dose of their own medicine. On June 8 he went forth toward the interior to make known the fact that he was there, and on this mission his troops captured nineteen guerrillas and an *alcalde*. They were returned to Perote where Walker "employed them in cleaning the streets and sinks." Remembering the Mier Expedition, at Camargo, Walker had let Mexican captives slice their feet to shreds on cactus; at Perote they were allowed to scrub the floors—and scrub, and scrub, and scrub. But mostly he did not take prisoners. By the end of the month, Oswandel was able to give an evaluation: "Should Capt. Walker come across the guerrillas God help them, for he seldom brings in prisoners. The Captain and most all of his men are very prejudiced and embittered against every guerrilla in the country."

The Battle of La Hoya Pass, fought on the morning of June 20, offers the outstanding single example of the type of service Walker's mounted riflemen rendered. His immediate commander was Colonel F. N. Wynkoop of the First Pennsylvania Volunteers. The problem was that a large American supply train was to go through that pass and the army knew that guerrillas were guarding it. Wynkoop had the job of clearing the field. Walker was detained at the small village of Las Vegas in a clean-up operation, but when he arrived at La Hoya in the early hours of the morning of June 20, the wagons were already under siege. Wynkoop was there but he did not attack until Walker arrived. Then he left it all to Walker's troopers.

Walker thought Wynkoop had a picket out, but he was mistaken. By the time he discovered the error the enemy was at his immediate front. Typically, he charged with such ferocity that the Mexicans were completely dislodged. None of Walker's men were wounded, so he followed the fleeing enemy. In the dark at full gallop the command ran headlong into a fence they could not see. Walker and eight men lost their horses to the fence, and some of the men were injured in the fall. Undaunted and unhurt, Walker found another horse as he continued in the lead.

When a force of five or six hundred Mexicans was encountered, another skirmish began. Walker, in his report to Wynkoop, described the scene:

> The moment was critical. Many of my men had never been under fire before, and nothing but my confidence in their heroic valor and coolness would have induced me to remain in my position. At this moment the men began to take their sabres from the fronts of their saddles, which had been secured in that way for the secret movements by night, and prepare to use them when it came to close quarters. The coolness and gallantry of my men, and the deadly crash of their rifles, soon convinced them it was better to retire. Their loss as near as I could judge, was at least forty killed and wounded. My whole force, including those injured in the charge, was fifty-one.

While Walker was doing the fighting, Wykoop had begun a retreat to Perote, but after Walker's troopers carried the fight, the colonel's men joined the mopping-up operations. The wagon train went through La Hoya Pass that day, but Walker never forgave Wynkoop for the retreat. It caused a rift between the two men that ended in Walker's spending one month "under arrest."

Late in the summer Walker took a force toward Jalapa where he caused the execution of several Mexicans who had been involved "in the murder of Americans." Then, in early September, Wynkoop had Walker arrested. The state of Walker's affairs at this time are best described in a letter he addressed to his brother Johnathan, at Washington. The captain wrote:

> Castle of Perote (Mexico)
> October 5th, 1847
> 10 P. M.
>
> Dear Brother
>
> I write in haste to inform you that I leave here tomorrow under command of General Lane in command of three other companies of Cavalry with the expectation of fighting Gen.

Santa Anna at the pass of Piñon about fifty miles from this place. He is said to have a force of eight thousand men. But I must confess that I have some doubts about his meeting us voluntarily our force being upwards of three thousand men. We will move light with as few wagons as possible.

A rumour has just reached us that Santa Anna has just left his position on the main road and gone to the City of Orizaba. In this event I think Gen. Lane will follow him untill he either fights or disperses his force, if we pass him he will probably pass down on the Orizaba Road to Vera Cruz and make some demonstrations against Vera Cruz or some other point on the line of our operation. Santa Anna seems determined not to make peace and seems disposed to continue the war under all circumstances. I look upon this determination as one of the most fortunate events that could transpire. As it will leave us the alternative of taking military possession of the country; which will finally result in the Annexation of Mexico and open a new and extensive field for the display of American genius and enterprise. I think Santa Anna's race is nearly run. Jack Hays will soon be here with his Regt. of Rangers and I have no doubt that Santa Anna will be in a tight place. If I had my revolving pistols I should feel strong hopes of capturing him or killing him. I have written three times to the different officers at Vera Cruz to forward them and two commands have come up since they arrived at Vera Cruz but I have no hope of getting them until Jack Hays comes up. I have allso made repeated applications to go for them but without success. My company however is well drilled in saber exercise and use the rifle very well. My company is reduced by deaths and discharges to seventy men but this is by far the largest number of effective men of any company in the service (of mounted men).

I have written to you several times giving you all particulars of matters and things in general but I doubt very much whether you have received anything from me or not, if not you will learn by the bearer of this everything of interest.

I shall forward allso by A. West who has been discharged for disability the amt. due Wesson for the Rifle which I have not heard of since you wrote to me about them and will forward you a draft for the amt. due you as soon as practicable. I have, however, almost made up my mind to send David home, as he is in bad health and has been for some time past, the result of home sickness in a great measure I have no doubt. He has been but little service to me thus far, and nothing but his honesty and attachment to me would induce me to keep him with me any longer. He desires to have his best wishes sent to you all. I gave him his choice to return home or go on with me. He says that he would like very well to go home but does not wish to leave me for fear something may happen to me.

I have just received a pair of Colts Pistols which he sent to me as a present, there is not an officer who has seen them but what speaks in the highest terms of them and all of the Cavalry officers are determined to get them if possible. Col. Harney says they are the best arm in the world. They are as effective as the common rifle at one hundred yards. Everybody is allso pleased with Wessons Rifle and are anxious to obtain them.

My love and best wishes to Mother and Relatives, Mr. Smith, and all enquiring friends and be assured of my high regards, etc., in haste.

S. H. Walker

To
    Johnathan T. Walker
      W. City
      D. C.

P. S. I have been one month under arrest by Col. F. N. Wynkoop the cowardly creature who was the first to retreat since the commencement of the war and that from an insignificant force of the enemy. Gen. Lane has ordered me to duty and given the command of three other companies not withstanding the Cols. protest. I asked for a court of enquiry which Gen. Lane would not grant for want of time.

Note the fact that Walker and his men did not yet have their Colt revolvers, that Walker received his pair of pistols on October 5, only four days before his death. Perhaps these weapons which came into his hands at a strategic moment gave him the added courage to seek the capture of Santa Anna as Walker had threatened.

The man to rescue Walker from the clutches of Wynkoop was General Joseph Lane, a soldier who knew how to handle a Texas Ranger. In his move to meet a large force reported to be at Puebla, he stopped at Perote. There he learned that Santa Anna himself commanded four thousand men and six artillery pieces at the town of Huamantla. Lane decided to pursue the famous Napoleon of the West and beard him in his own den. Walker responded happily to that idea. His Rangers, as they were called throughout the war, led the charge. Lane instructed Walker to move ahead of the column but to stay within supportable distance. This Walker did not do; his companions say that he was obsessed with the thought of capturing Santa Anna.

When Walker was within three miles of the town, he ordered a gallop. Over ditches and ruts the horses ran into the city. Walker ordered a trot, moving by twos, until the lane opened into the main street leading to the plaza. The troop was reformed into a column of four as Walker gave the order "draw sabres and charge." One soldier reminisced about the scene, one which recalls the charge of Hays' Rangers against the Indians, as he wrote: "Then rose a wild yell, and such a charge! The flashing of the sabres, the thundering of the horses' feet over the paved streets, were enough to strike terror into the hearts of the enmy." Up the street they saw Mexican soldiers preparing two artillery pieces for battle. After taking the cannon, Walker's men engaged the enemy for forty-five minutes before the remainder of Lane's troops could catch up. The fighting ended successfully for the Americans; Santa Anna had fought his last battle, but so had Sam Walker.

Wallace's servant, David, had died in the battle while saving the life of Surgeon John T. Lamar of Georgia. Walker was killed as he was moving to a churchyard surrounded by a high wall. Some reports say he was shot in the head, others that the ball entered the left shoulder from the back and passed above the heart. Lane, in his official report to the Adjutant General, took note of Walker's death: "This victory is saddened by the loss of one of the most chivalric, noble-hearted men that graced the profession of arms—Captain Samuel H. Walker, of the mounted riflemen. Foremost in the advance, he had routed the enemy when he fell mortally wounded. In his death, the service has met with a loss which cannot easily be repaired." Colonel Wynkoop, when he heard that the Ranger was wounded, hurried to Walker's side as though an urgent message needed to be imparted, but Wynkoop arrived too late.

The bodies of Walker and David were returned to Perote by November 5 at the order of Wynkoop with the intent of forwarding them to the United States. This apparently was not accomplished immediately. In the fall of 1848, Walker's remains passed through Austin on their way to San Antonio for burial. At Austin, the event precipitated a procession of civil and military officials and citizens. A salute to Walker was fired from President Hill.

On the twentieth anniversary of the Battle of San Jacinto, on April 21, 1856, a large crowd gathered at San Antonio to witness the re-interment of two of the best Texas Rangers of all time. Under the auspices of the Independent Order of Odd-Fellows, Samuel Hamilton Walker and Richard Addison Gillespie were laid side by side; they remain there today. Orator for the occasion was James C. Wilson, the same man who had escaped out of Mexico with Walker in 1843. Wilson had become a Methodist preacher and he took especial pains to point out the fact that Sam Walker was a courageous, moral person. He knew well the temper of the man. In the oratory style of the day, Wilson proclaimed:

> Walker in ordinary service seemed quite an ordinary man; retiring, silent, mild, apathetic, and rather melancholy, performing his duties merely from a sense of duty, and not that he delighted in them; yet never failing to perform them well. . . . In action, . . . Walker was rapid, untiring, terrible. Like Cameron he seemed to change his whole character and appearance and arise a new being, entirely superior to himself. . . . Walker had no sense of fear. . . . Walker seemed to seek danger; to love it for himself. . . . Walker was a hero.

The eulogy at San Antonio was a belated one. Actually, the laurels came much earlier and over a broader expanse than Texas. Walker's death in 1847 made a distinct impact on New Orleans, Baltimore, Washington, and New York. *The Spirit of the Times* pointed to Walker's international reputation and noted the "melancholy sensation" the event caused in New York. *Niles National Register* kept the people of Baltimore well informed on affairs concerning Walker's remains. He was commemorated in prose, poetry, and drama. When the *Rough and Ready Almanacs,* published in 1847 and 1848, pictured him as a superman, the writer was merely following the script of a drama entitled, *The Campaign on the Rio Grande or Triumphs in Mexico* which was popular on Broadway in 1846. The play had Sam Walker as the leading character. As late as February 1850, *Graham's Magazine* printed a poem about Walker which read:

> For a braver, or a better, or a more chivalrous knight
> Never put his lance in rest in the days when might was right;
> And he had the fox's cunning, and the eagle's restless eye,
> With his courage, to see danger, and that danger to defy.

In Texas, on September 28, 1853, the *Texas Monument* at La Grange printed an article by Jack Humphries entitled "Who Killed Captain Walker! A Thrilling Episode of the Mexican War." The editor had pirated the article from the *New York Dutchman* and he allotted it fully one-half of the front page. When Walker County, Texas, was created in 1846, the legislators named it in honor of Robert J. Walker of Mississippi; however, as the Civil War progressed R. J. Walker emerged a Unionist, so in 1863 the Texas Legislature decreed that the county "should be named to honor the memory of Captain Samuel H. Walker, of the Texas Ranger Service, who fell in Mexico."

So Sam Walker was considered a Texas Ranger from the time he hit Texas until his death. He did service in the United States Army and perhaps had his most glorious moments in that uniform, but he always did so as a Texas Ranger—using Ranger tactics to fight Ranger style. In every sense of the word, Walker was one of Jack Hays' boys. He could have earned no more fitting tribute than that.

Ben McCulloch

Ben McCulloch scouts a Mexican Army Camp -- February, 1847

Ben McCulloch

by

Ben Procter

The Texas Rangers have always been a special breed of men, persevering and persistent, physically tough, rugged in temperament and spirit. Since 1835 they have expected, indeed demanded, that each member be the personification of fearlessness and devotion to duty. No matter what the odds, they have been forced by tradition to seek out the enemy, to advance with the intent of overwhelming or destroying them, to be worthy of the phrase, "One Riot! One Ranger!"

Although highly esteemed by Texans during Republic days, the Rangers did not achieve national fame and recognition until the Mexican War. Their unconventional dress and tactics, their skill with a horse and gun, their unbelievable fierceness and at times brutality, amazed and awed the Mexicans. Out of respect or fear they were called "diablos Tejanos"—the Texas devils. And no wonder! John S. "Rip" Ford, after watching their daily military performances in 1846 for General Zachary Taylor, admiringly remarked: "They ride like Mexicans; trail like Indians; shoot like Tennesseans; and fight like the devil."

In looks and manner the Rangers were easily distinguishable from the rest of the American army that invaded Mexico. Bearded and unkempt, "dressed in every variety of garment, with one exception, the slouched hat," armed to the teeth with knives, a rifle, and a brace of Walker five-shooters, they had a "ferocious and outlaw look." In fact, the only well-groomed "critters" in their camp were horses, magnificent animals which the Rangers religiously cared for. Nowhere was there evidence of the military—no flags or pennants, no insignias or evidences of rank, no formality between officers and enlisted men.

Yet there was no mistaking a Ranger captain. He had a charismatic quality that set him apart from his men. Although not necessarily large or powerful physically, he exuded a quiet confidence. Almost instinctively in a time of crisis he knew what to do, possessing that rare combination of boldness and judgment which allowed him, as Walter Prescott Webb observed, "to lead rather than direct his men." For him, retreat was unpardonable, defeat unbearable; his reputation and prestige demanded success.

Ben McCulloch was one of the first men who helped cast the mold for a Ranger captain, who typified invincible leadership. Born on November 11, 1811, in Rutherford County, Tennessee, he inherited a family tradition of modest, inconspicuous living, of being part of the mass migration which conquered the American wilderness. Even though the family tree is hazy, his great-great-grandfather, Benjamin, probably arrived from Ireland early in the eighteenth century. For almost a hundred years the McCullochs lived in Virginia, leading a normal life, tilling the soil, raising a little corn and lots of children. By the nineteenth century Alexander McCulloch, Ben's father, had migrated to Tennessee and in the War of 1812 had achieved enough public stature to become aide-de-camp to General John C. Coffee. Then he served under Andrew Jackson at the battles of Horseshoe Bend and New Orleans.

One of twelve children, Ben McCulloch spent his youth in a manner typical of frontier America. Soon after his family moved to northern Alabama in 1820, he was called upon to help in the fields. Like so many pioneer boys of his day, he received little education, only two months of formal schooling; but he learned to read, especially the Bible, since all of the family were active members of the Methodist Episcopal Church. As was often the case with such young men, he longed for an education and, if folklore and legend are correct, spent many hours straining to read by campfire or pineknot light. Such ambition, however, did not deter him from excelling in forest craft, from learning the ways of the nearby Choctaws, from becoming an avid fisherman and a skilled hunter. In fact, he was so proficient with a rifle that his father assigned him the task of providing meat for the family; one season he reportedly killed eighty bears.

Early in 1830 Alexander McCulloch moved once again, this time to Dyer County in western Tennessee. And for young Ben such a move opened up new worlds. With the Mississippi River only a few miles distant he could travel to unknown lands rather easily, see such fascinating places as St. Louis and New Orleans, perhaps put this extraordinary hunting skills to better use. Although only nineteen, he had already gained recognition as a "natural woodsman." In 1832, after trying unsuccessfully to join a Santa Fe trading expedition, he visited the rough and boisterous lead-mining towns along the Upper Mississippi River Valley; from 1833 to 1835 he and his brother, Henry, floated log rafts down the Mississippi to Natchez and markets farther south; while between these economic ventures, he continued to hunt, having found a close companion and kindred spirit of equal skill, Congressman Davy Crockett.

In the fall of 1835, however, McCulloch changed the direction of his life. With the Texas Revolution mounting in intensity he agreed to join Crockett, who had just been defeated for re-election, in fighting the Mexicans. Such a plan, adventuresome and challenging, appealed to him. Since both had private and business affairs to wind up, they decided to rendezvous at Nacogdoches on December 25 and celebrate Christmas by feasting "off the hump of a buffalo."

Yet their plans never materialized; McCulloch never saw his comrade again. Because of pressing family responsibilities he was unable to reach Texas until January, 1836. By then, Crockett had already left for San Antonio. Several days later McCulloch pressed on, hoping to catch up with him. At the Brazos River he came down with the measles and, by the time that he had recovered, Mexican forces under General Antonio Lopez de Santa Anna were besieging the Alamo. On March 6, after a furious and heroic defense, the embattled Crockett and his fellow Tennesseans were finally overrun by a swarm of Mexican infantrymen.

For the next ten weeks Texans witnessed and participated in what was known as the "Runaway Scrape." After Santa Anna raised the blood-red flag at the Alamo (signifying "no quarter") and while Colonel James Fannin and his men "were shot down like dogs" near Goliad, they fled eastward from Gonzales before a victorious Mexican army. What a bitter march it was. Each day they applied a scorched-earth policy to their homes and farm lands; each step backward galled them because they were retreating before the enemy instead of avenging their fallen comrades.

Ben McCulloch also participated in this hectic, undisciplined flight. But in comparison with those who had left from Gonzales his experiences were far less harrowing and much more rewarding. Early in April at Groce's Crossing, Houston welcomed him into his mud-spattered, grumbling army, almost immediately placing him in charge of the "Twin Sisters," two newly arrived cannon which the citizens of Cincinnati had donated for the defense of the Republic. For two weeks the Texans continued their retreat southward toward Harrisburg near Buffalo Bayou and the San Jacinto River. There on April 21 they stopped, turned, and struck back at their hated pursuers, at last releasing their pent-up emotions and frustrations. Now it was "Remember the Alamo, Remember Goliad!"—and victory.

Although promoted to first lieutenant after the Battle of San Jacinto, McCulloch soon realized that army life was not for him. The inactivity, the boredom, the seemingly endless routine was deadening, especially for someone of his temperament and background. To break the monotony he first obtained a furlough to explore the frontier along the Lavaca and

Guadalupe rivers. Upon returning, he quickly volunteered to raise army recruits in Tennessee; by the fall of 1836 he had gathered together thirty enlistees. But the tedium of army life overcame him, so he terminated his service.

McCulloch spent the next year searching for the right profession, for that area of the country where he really belonged. Briefly he explored the frontier again but could reach no decision. Then during the winter of 1837 he worked in Houston as a carpenter until at length, still dissatisfied, he returned to Tennessee specifically to learn surveying from his father. After all, with the Texas Land Office opening in February, 1838, the Republic would need men professionally skilled in laying out plots, yet who could survive in the wilderness.

For his base of operation McCulloch chose historic Gonzales—and for good reason. It suited his character. Surely the action was there, the violence and impending danger of the frontier, the mystery and solitude of a sparsely-settled region. Besides, he could combine surveying with his extraordinary hunting talents.

In this instance, however, the quarry was far more dangerous than bear, for the citizens of Gonzales were under continual Indian alert. So the task of defense, of punishment, of seeking out and destroying, fell heavily upon such men as Ben McCulloch and his brother, Henry. And because of their particular training and experience, they proved equal to every crisis. Time and again during 1838 and 1839 they alerted the settlers against attack. Just as frequently they fought running skirmishes with the raiders, while occasionally they surprised and cut them to pieces, as at Peach Creek in March, 1839.

But these actions were merely defensive, fighting or counterattacking after being surprised, almost like a rear-guard action; in no way did such measures remove the Indian menace. In fact, the Comanches became much more brazen in 1840, stealing and killing indiscriminately. Incensed and outraged when some of their chiefs were slain at a peace parley in San Antonio (the Council House Fight), approximately 1,000 warriors swept across Texas early in August, striking isolated districts near Gonzales, attacking Victoria, then sacking and burning Linnville on Matagorda Island.

To meet this bloody invasion the Texans mobilized quickly. Having seen evidences of Comanche vengeance and barbarity, their fiendish use of the knife, their agonizingly slow torture by fire, their senseless murder of women and children, they were determined to exact a fitting retribution, to inflict so much destruction and punishment that the Comanches would always remember. Immediately McCulloch marched from Gonzales with twenty-four men to join Captain John L. Tumlinson and approximately one hundred Victoria militia. On August 9 they encountered the enemy at the Casa Blanca River, but after a brief skirmish Tumlinson, who commanded the larger force, decided that a full-scale battle would be too risky and allowed the Indians to pass.

What a disheartening, bitter turn of events! McCulloch was furious. After observing the Indians closely, their movements and actions, he was convinced that they were trying to avoid a fight, that a surprise frontal assault would have routed them. Unable to abide by Tumlinson's decision, he left with three companions, loudly voicing his disgust and unhappiness at being overruled, angrily vowing that he was going to seek action elsewhere. In fact, he had already heard rumors that other groups of Texans were gathering at Plum Creek. Surely they would demand a direct confrontation.

In this assumption he was correct. For at Plum Creek the Texans were in complete agreement, determined not to let the savages return northward unscathed. Captain Matthew Caldwell, also of Gonzales, reflected the feelings of those assembled when he announced: "Boys, the Indians number about one thousand. They have our women and children captives. We are only eighty-seven, but I believe we can whip hell out of 'em."

And that was exactly what they did. When the Comanches neared the creek crossing on August 12, the Texans, reinforced and now numbering more than 200, blocked their path. While one obviously important chief, magnificent in a feathered headdress, paraded imperiously before them, McCulloch and Caldwell and Colonel Edward Burleson who recognized this act of bravado as a delaying tactic urged General Felix Houston, newly arrived and somewhat unsure of himself, to order a charge. Within a few minutes they had their wish—shots rang out; the befeathered chief fell mortally wounded; and the Texans urged their mounts forward, scattering the startled Indians. For ten to twelve miles a running battle occurred, with each man seeking his own personal vengeance. And when their bloody work was done, they had killed at least eighty-six Comanches as compared to their own losses of one dead and seven wounded.

After Plum Creek McCulloch was recognized widely as a fearless soldier, as a man to rely upon in troublesome times, as a resourceful frontiersman who knew how to deal with Texas' enemies. Throughout 1840 and 1841, therefore, he was constantly on call, pursuing and attacking raiders or patrolling areas where Indian signs were prevalent. So violent did the situation on the Gonzales frontier become, so horrible the depredations, that from July 11 to December 18, 1841, he enlisted in a group of minute-men, mounted riflemen who were ready for "any emergency."

Even more dangerous, however, was the enemy to the south, for the Mexicans would not recognize Texas independence. So inevitably McCulloch would encounter them, the result being that as his knowledge of them increased, his hatred grew. In March, 1842, after the Santa Fe Expedition had failed miserably, the Mexicans retaliated by capturing San Antonio. Unsuccessful, their army forced to retreat after only two days, they invaded again in September. On both occasions McCulloch served as a scout for the Texas forces, infiltrating enemy lines, noting troop concentrations and the amount of supplies, and finding out what the Mexicans planned to do. Then he joined Captain John C. "Jack" Hays and his Rangers in driving the invaders back to the Rio Grande. Fortunately neither man remained with the ill-fated Mier Expedition. Yet McCulloch, like all Texans, would remember what happened to those 300 men the Mexicans captured, the starvation and brutality, the almost unbelievable hardships, and particularly the inhuman lottery of drawing the black bean of death.

Nor did these bitter memories in any way subside during the next three years. While fighting under Captain Jack Hays and working his way to second-in-command in the Rangers, he uncovered conclusive evidence that the Mexicans were encouraging and abetting Comanche raids or were themselves moving northward from the Rio Grande to rob and kill. Even in 1845 while serving in the First Legislature of Texas, he had cause to remember; Mexican opposition to the annexation of Texas was obvious. And also just as obvious was the fact that men like McCulloch were ready to eliminate Mexico as a constant threat, thereby settling once and for all the question of independence.

In March, 1846, after President James K. Polk ordered General Zachary "Old Rough and Ready" Taylor to the Rio Grande, Texans got their wish. Within six weeks "American blood had been shed upon American soil"—the war had begun. Immediately McCulloch resigned from the Legislature, returned to Gonzales and recruited a Ranger company, and by May 13 was riding southward toward the Rio Grande. Six days later he and his men arrived at Point Isabel, then proceeded to Fort Brown opposite Matamoros, and offered their services to General Taylor.

What a welcome addition they were. Together with the Ranger companies captained by Jack Hays, Samuel Walker, Richard Gillespie, and John Price, they became the eyes and ears of the American army. And apparently they were the best soldiers; at least Taylor seemed to favor them. For besides being superbly mounted and armed and equipped, they had a captain who inspired confidence, indeed commanded it. Almost thirty-five at the time, McCulloch looked the part of a "partisan leader." His weather-beaten face, tanned and leathered by the sun and wind, his deep-set eyes made even more striking because of a high, broad forehead and a large, straight nose, formed a mask, indicating no emotions, betraying no thoughts or intentions. Experienced and proven, he seemed to be at his best when in danger, his reflexes and thinking automatically quickening. And even though slightly under six feet, lithe and thinly muscled, he was completely color-blind to fear.

For more than three weeks McCulloch and his men impatiently awaited orders, each day of idleness causing increased grumbling and restlessness. That they endured such inactivity stoically was somewhat surprising, that they maintained good behavior, keeping in check their violent nature, seemed almost unbelievable, especially under such abominable conditions. While obviously unhappy over having missed their chance to participate in the recent American victories at Palo Alto and Resaca de la Palma on May 8-9, they were even more disgruntled at having to camp in that particular area. If the swarms of mosquitoes failed to keep them awake at night, the stench of rotting flesh or the presence of ravenous wolves and carrion birds succeeded. For that matter, the days were no better. The hot sun blistered them in this inhospitable land; sudden thundershowers soaked them to the skin; a humid, sweltering climate made them feel uncomfortable, the ever-present dust adhering to their sticky, perspiring bodies like a second layer of skin. Nor were they well provided for—tents, cooking utensils, camp equipage were all in short supply. "Whether it was because they thought the Texan troops were accustomed to, and could endure more hardships than any other troops in the field, we do not know," Sam Reid, one of McCulloch's men, reflected. But "one thing is certain. They gave us ... ample ... opportunity to evince our greatest powers of endurance and fortitude."

No wonder the Rangers welcomed orders from General Taylor on June 12, no wonder they were eager to scout the rugged terrain toward Linares. Selecting thirty-nine men, McCulloch moved across the Rio Grande, through Matamoros, and out into a desolate, arid countryside. With each mile, with each day, he gained both in stature and respect. Obviously a skilled scout, a master at deception, at understanding the Mexican mind, he continued to amaze his company with unusual cunning and strategy. To prevent enemy spies from discovering his purpose he first traveled the Reynosa road, then swung over to the Linares route. Whenever possible he would circle a settlement or rancho, approaching it from the west to give the impression that the Rangers were moving toward Matamoros from Monterrey. Upon deciding to attack, he would "strike like a bullet, suddenly and with little warning." In the ensuing encounter he and his men, intense Mexican-haters, convinced that the army policy of conciliating the populace was "absurd," were brutal and unrelenting, seldom taking anyone alive. Of course, McCulloch easily justified such actions in his own mind. After all, in ranging swiftly over enemy territory, he could ill afford the luxury of taking prisoners who would hamper his activities, hence effectiveness.

Onward the Rangers rode toward Linares, oftentimes jesting and laughing, Sam Reid recalled, like a group "gayly trooping to a wedding or a fair." Because of the torturous terrain and the fierce weather McCulloch lost five men in three days to sickness and injury; yet the worst part was still ahead. By June 20 he was within sixty miles of Linares and already he knew that the route was not "practicable" for Taylor to use. But it was rumored that General Antonio Canales, the "Chaparral Fox," was nearby, and McCulloch "most desired" to capture this butcher who had brutalized friends and fellow Texans at Mier in 1842, who had executed one out of ten prisoners. No matter that the Rangers were without food for two days, that the country became wilder and more unbearable, that the sun, blazing down from a cloudless, steel-blue sky, was pitilessly "scorching and roasting" them. No one wanted to miss a chance at Canales. By June 21, however, their situation became desperate, their suffering almost intolerable; they must have water for both themselves and their animals—or die. So the orders went out to "scatter" and "find a waterhole." Just before sundown one Ranger, yelling jubilantly, announced that he had discovered one "about half a mile to the right." The rush was on. "Helter-skelter, without order," the men raced to quench their thirst. But when they arrived, McCulloch loomed ominously before them with guns drawn, "threatening to shoot the first man who rode into the pond." Dutifully they obeyed, drinking slowly and filling their canteens before letting their horses and pack animals plunge in and muddy the water.

All the next day the Rangers rode leisurely toward Reynosa, having learned that Canales was no longer within striking distance. After ten days of arduous scouting across 100 miles of enemy territory, they had acquitted themselves admirably, so well in fact that they were already becoming a legend. The Mexicans were not the only ones awed by them; for as they rode into Reynosa, George Kendall of the *New Orleans Picayune* remarked: "I have seen a goodly number of volunteers in my time, but Capt. McCulloch's men are choice specimens."

For the next five weeks the Rangers idled while the American army caught up with them; yet they found outlets for their explosive energies and rugged talents. On several occasions they relieved their monotony by volunteering for patrols, once trying to capture Mexican bandits, another time tracking the marauding Comanches for five days. But their principal concern was the attitude of the Reynosa inhabitants who were derisive, even hostile; therefore, the Rangers employed their own unique methods of correcting what they considered a bad situation. In regard to stories that General Canales and Colonel Juan Seguin, a former Texas patriot, were going to attack one night soon and slit their throats, they were openly contemptuous, welcoming a confrontation. To justify this attitude they demonstrated whenever possible their superior physical prowess and expert horsemanship, their best opportunity being the Mexican game called the "chicken race" whereby a Ranger, riding full speed, would hang from his saddle, grab a chicken, and invariably outdistance all local adversaries to an appointed goal. They marked for special attention, however, those "greasers" who remained unconvinced and who foolishly stirred up the populace against them. Of course, they followed military orders which explicitly forbade the molesting of unarmed citizenry; but even so, Sam Reid noted, some of the more vocal troublemakers "were found shot or hung up in the chaparral." And what was the Rangers' explanation? Most probably these villains, "tortured by conscience for the many evil deeds they had committed, . . . had recklessly laid violent hands upon their own lives! "Quien sabe?' "

At last on August 1 the waiting ended; orders arrived for the Rangers to move out. And once again they had been chosen to point the way, for Taylor expected McCulloch to find the best route for the American army. He was not disappointed. For three days the Rangers reconnoitered the countryside leading to the small village of China which, like the Linares area, proved to be unsuitable and inhospitable. Then, after unsuccessfully trying to capture Colonel Seguin, they returned to Reynosa. By August 12 they were again on reconnaissance, this time investigating the road to Mier. After five days McCulloch reported to Taylor that this route was by far the most favorable.

So immediately the American advance commenced; now the cry was "On to Monterrey." Slowly, cautiously, methodically—that was the Taylor technique—the army moved deeper into Mexico, thereby hoping to precipitate a large-scale battle. Each day evidence that a direct confrontation would soon take place became increasingly apparent. Sleepy, isolated villages, inhabited by a phlegmatic populace and hundreds of yelping dogs, were now ominously silent. Along the route Mexican merchants, who in the past would have been overjoyed by the prospects of enormous profits, were morose and unapproachable, probably because General Pedro de Ampudia had issued a proclamation threatening death to anyone giving comfort to the invaders. At the same time, spies whom McCulloch and his men had captured for questioning were telling stories of heightening Mexican patriotism, of staunch resistance, of firm resolve. In fact, throughout the American ranks, from officers to enlisted men, rumors that a huge Mexican force was gathering either at Saltillo or Monterrey, that wealthy rancheros were uniting with poor peons to defend their country, were the order of the day. In one respect all the reports were the same—the Americans would not advance with impunity; they would encounter fierce opposition.

Actually the only effect of these rumors was to excite the Rangers, Reid recalled, and put them "in high spirits." With great anticipation they prepared for battle, constantly cleaning and oiling their guns. After all, to fight "greasers" was why they were here and what they had been waiting for. As the army neared Monterrey, they increased their scouting activities, eagerly looking forward to "a brush with the enemy."

On September 14 they got their wish—and McCulloch was at his best. While reconnoitering that morning with fifteen men he came upon the fresh trail of a Mexican cavalry unit. After a mile of tracking he found about eighty of them deployed on an opposing hill. Brandishing his sword "as if motioning to an army in the rear," he surprised them with a straight frontal assault and drove them from their position. Soon thereafter he discovered another body of enemy soldiers ready to ambush several Americans, so again he repeated this maneuver and once again was successful.

Now the fighting became more intense, the resistance more concentrated. But it did not matter. McCulloch and his Rangers had drawn first blood. Near the small village of Ramos they encountered both infantry and lancers, 200 strong, well-fortified and ready for a stand. Unslinging their rifles while dismounting, they poured a withering fire into the enemy ranks. Then as the Mexicans, demoralized by such devastating marksmanship, broke and ran, McCulloch ordered his company of forty men to charge, to pursue and give no quarter. After a running fight of six miles he finally discontinued the attack and retired, fully satisfied with the day's results.

During the next few days the Rangers were "like boys at play," Luther Giddings of the First Ohio Volunteers marveled, riding recklessly beneath the outer walls of Monterrey, daring the Mexicans to shoot, and deriding them for missing. Yet despite such antics and horseplay Taylor ordered Gillespie and McCulloch and Hays to lead the way on September 19 when he mounted an attack. For no matter what else might be said about him, "Old Rough and Ready" knew his men and what they could do. The Rangers were superb shock troops; they would devastate the enemy.

Consequently the taking of Monterrey was never in doubt, because the Rangers, after two days of light skirmishing, set the tempo and style of battle. On September 21 at the Hacienda of San Jeronimo they suddenly came upon 1,500 Mexicans, mostly lancers supported by infantrymen, brilliant in their uniforms, their highly-polished lances glistening in the sun, their horses spirited and prancing, readying for a charge. Immediately General William J. Worth ordered the Rangers forward to occupy a position along a wooden fence and withstand the anticipated assault. But McCulloch, far out in front, not hearing the command to dismount and hold (or not wishing to), urged his men to meet force with more force and thereby stymie the enemy attack. Galloping at full speed, they charged the lancers, led by Lieutenant Colonel Juan Nájera, head-on. Then the slaughter began. With deadly thoroughness the Rangers fought at close range, firing their pistols point-blank, stunning the Mexicans with shotgun blasts, using knives and swords with deadly effectiveness. Down went Nájera, glassy-eyed in death; fallen also were most of the lancers who had ridden beside him, their empty saddles stark evidence of what was happening. Forward the Rangers continued to surge, their larger mounts rocking and jarring the smaller Mexican steeds backwards. At one point in the fighting McCulloch with a few of his men suddenly realized that they had penetrated too far, that the enemy was closing behind them; so quickly they whirled about and cut their way out of encirclement. After fifteen minutes of such carnage the Mexicans fled unceremoniously, shattered and beaten, leaving behind 150 dead.

From this defeat the Mexican forces never recovered. The Americans had the momentum; they refused to relinquish it. For three days the Rangers performed incredibly, storming every enemy stronghold, overcoming every obstacle. Federation Hill and Fort Soldada! Independence Hill and the Bishop's Palace! All succumbed to their onslaught. Then the fighting degenerated to house-to-house combat, and the Rangers, if possible, were even more effective. Indian style, they swept through the city until on September 24 General Ampudia, under a flag of truce, begged for a suspension of hostilities.

When Taylor proclaimed an eight-week armistice after Ampudia agreed to evacuate Monterrey, the Rangers decided to go home, their enlistments having expired. After all, they had come "to fight, not to parley." Upon discharging them, Taylor praised their reckless bravery and unique abilities as fighting men; yet, in reality, he was happy to see them depart. For during the week of negotiations following the battle, they displayed, Giddings remarked, a "lawless and vindictive spirit"—in other words, no Mexican was safe. And Taylor did not relish the thought of policing 1,000 Texas Rangers, of trying to keep them occupied for two months.

So in October, 1846, McCulloch and sixteen of his company left Monterrey for Matamoros, San Antonio, and home—but not for long. Before departing, he had agreed to return "in case hostilities should be commenced" and if needed. By the end of the year it was apparent that his services would be required. Negotiations had hopelessly disintegrated. Already Taylor had occupied Saltillo and Victoria after having notified Santa Anna, the new Mexican commander, that peace for the moment was an illusion. Yet, regarding the American military operations, "Old Rough and Ready" had become increasingly dissatisfied and even alarmed. Without the Rangers as scouts, he was hesitant, even insecure, at times having to make decisions without adequate knowledge and information. Since December the Mexicans had captured and brutalized his couriers, intercepted messages to and from him, ambushed patrols, and dominated the countryside. Where was McCulloch? For over a month he had asked for him repeatedly.

On February 4, 1847, Ben McCulloch, recently promoted to major, arrived in Saltillo with twenty-seven men and was immediately pressed into service, but not until Taylor agreed to enlist them for only six months (army regulations specified a minimum of a year). And what were his orders? Simply complete a mission in which all others had failed. Cross the desert to Encarnacion, a large rancho approximately thirty miles distant, find out what the Mexican army was preparing to do, and return.

To carry out this hazardous patrol McCulloch selected sixteen particularly tough Rangers. On February 16 they vanished into the dense chaparral and cactus, finally emerging at 11 p.m. about a mile from their destination. With the night almost pitch-black McCulloch, unsure of his bearings, decided to follow a main road. Then "within thirty paces" he suddenly came upon at least twenty enemy horsemen. Almost instinctively he ordered his men to charge, thereby giving the impression in the darkness that a superior force was attacking. After a brief running skirmish he regrouped his men and returned to Agua Nuéva, Taylor's new headquarters. In his report he estimated that there were possibly 1,500 lancers at Encarnacion.

Approximation, however, was not good enough for Taylor. It was rumored that Santa Anna was moving up, which, of course, meant that a battle was pending; and a worried Taylor had no specific information on which to make a decision. So on February 20 McCulloch had to return to Encarnacion, and this time he was determined to gain detailed intelligence on Santa Anna's advance.

Although slightly alttering his plan of operations, McCulloch still relied upon his cunning and unfailing instincts. To reduce the probability of detection he chose a smaller group, only six men, and then moved out at 4:00 that afternoon, partly because of the heat and lack of water en route. After six miles they captured—and sent to Taylor—a Mexican deserter who claimed that Santa Anna had just arrived at Encarnacion with 20,000 men. But this information needed to be substantiated; the Mexican mind thrived on rumors and overstatement. Onward they pressed through a lonely, forlorn country, the thorny chaparral and cactus reaching out and tearing at them; yet McCulloch, even in the darkness, would not chance the easier route along the main road. Near midnight they finally reached the outer perimeter of Encarnacion—and there encamped in force was the Mexican army.

Quickly, but with extreme caution, the Rangers carried out their assignment. Stealthily they moved past the outer guard of sentries, the darkness sheathing and protecting them. Despite the danger McCulloch ordered his men to scout the perimeters of the encampment, thereby determining more correctly the size of the army. Within an hour they rendezvoused as planned, whereupon McCulloch dispatched Lieutenant Fielding Alston and four Rangers to report to General Taylor.

Meanwhile McCulloch decided to remain behind. And why? Most likely he was reluctant to face Taylor again without the fullest information. Or perhaps he was determined that there would not be a third reconnaissance to Encarnacion. In any case, he was in the midst of the enemy, with only one man accompanying him, fully cognizant that capture would mean torture and death. So for the moment he needed to find both an observation post and a place of safety. But as the two men groped in the darkness, a sentry challenged them. To avoid detection they instinctively spurred their horses toward the center of the camp, thereby hoping to pass as Mexican cavalry returning from patrol. Then luckily they chanced upon a perfect hiding place, a wood-covered hill approximately a mile from the main force. Relieved and exhausted, they fell asleep.

It was just at daybreak on February 21 when the racket from beating drums and blaring trumpets, signifying reveille, awakened the two

Rangers. As they carefully peered from their vantage point, the Mexican camp unfolded before them. And what an impressive, indeed picturesque sight it was—men and animals beginning to stir about; smoke from hundreds of green-wood fires curling lazily skyward, at times almost obscuring the view; soldiers readying themselves for the forthcoming day.

After surveying the camp and realizing that his nighttime estimate had been fairly accurate, McCulloch now had to devise an escape. With the enemy all about, only one solution seemed plausible. Characteristic of the man, it was both bold and daring, its success hinging upon surprise and the unexpected. He and his fellow Ranger must try to impersonate Mexican cavalrymen, relaxed and unconcerned, carrying out their daily assignments. Consequently they rode nonchalantly onto the main road leading out of Encarnacion, passed within a few feet of several sentries, and then, upon clearing the outer perimeter, galloped swiftly toward the American lines.

Unknown to them, however, General Taylor, acting on the information received the previous night, was already pulling his forces back from Agua Nuéva to a much more defensible position near the Hacienda of Buena Vista. Yet anxiously he awaited McCulloch's return to have his decision confirmed. When the Ranger dashed into camp, Taylor held an immediate audience. After listening intently and at length to the detailed report about the Mexican army, he was no longer disturbed that Santa Anna was advancing. "Very well, Major, that's all I wanted to know," he announced. "I am glad they did not catch you." Then confidently he rode to Buena Vista and the next day won his most memorable victory.

Soon thereafter McCulloch resigned his commission as major and returned home a national hero. But being a man of action, of restless energy, nurtured by adventure and thriving on danger, he could not settle down. After the federal government denied his petition in 1849 for a colonelcy in the United States cavalry, he joined the mad rush of the Forty-Niners to California, his most cherished dream having eluded him. Yet for four years, instead of panning gold, he served as sheriff of Sacramento County, carrying out this hazardous duty with his usual thoroughness. In 1853 he returned to Texas as federal marshal of the Eastern District, with his headquarters at Galveston. Then in 1858, with the Mormons threatening war in Utah, he and former governor of Kentucky L. W. Powell were appointed by President James Buchanan as peace commissioners. After a long journey to Salt Lake City and a short conference with Brigham Young, they settled the dispute satisfactorily.

Resigning as federal marshal on April 1, 1859, McCulloch was briefly an agent for an arms manufacturer, astounding customers and spectators with demonstrations of marksmanship. But with slavery and secession becoming paramount in the United States in 1861, he offered his services to the Confederacy. In Texas the Committee on Public Safety appointed him as a colonel of cavalry and on February 9 ordered him to San Antonio, specifically to obtain the surrender of all Federal forces. When he arrived six days later with 400 men, Major General David E. Twiggs, the commandant of the Eighth District, promptly surrendered. For his next assignment the Committee sent him to Virginia to purchase 2,000 Colt revolvers and Morse rifles, but this time he was unsuccessful. Then on May 11 the Confederate Congress commissioned him a brigadier general, assigning him to the Indian Territory. Within two months he had rejuvenated Confederate morale west of the Mississippi, defeating the Federal forces at Wilson's Creek rather easily. But on March 7, 1862, he was not so fortunate. At the Battle of Pea Ridge while he was reconnoittering an enemy position which had been particularly troublesome, sniper-fire cut him down.

News of his death saddened Texans. Gone was one of their true heroes, a man who had fought for their independence, who had protected them from red savages and brown invaders, who had helped bring civilization to an inhospitable wilderness. To them he personified that indomitable spirit which had been responsible for establishing a Republic and then a state—a Texas Ranger, scouting from a hill overlooking the Mexican encampment at Encarnacion, who was willing to risk capture, torture, and death so that Zachary Taylor could achieve an American victory.

John Salmon (Rip) Ford

John S. "Rip" Ford, death of Iron Jacket -- May 12, 1858

John Salmon (Rip) Ford

by

HAROLD B. SIMPSON

Late in 1847, during the Mexican War, the adjutant of the First Regiment of Texas Mounted Volunteers (Rangers) sat down at a crude desk at headquarters to carry out one of the least desirable duties of his office. The regiment, proceeding from Vera Cruz to Mexico City, had been constantly harassed by Mexican guerrilla forces and had sustained several casualties. By custom, the next-of-kin of those killed were to be notified by the regimental adjutant. The erect, lean adjutant of Colonel John Coffee (Jack) Hays' Regiment, in reverence for the dead, closed his letters of notification and condolence with the expression "Rest in Peace." As the regiment drew closer to the capital city, Mexican irregulars stepped up their attacks and the Texas casualties mounted. Captain Ford, seeking to reduce the time spent on paperwork, shortened his benevolent ending to "R.I.P." A fellow Ranger, noting the abbreviated expression, immediately tabbed the adjutant "Old Rip"—a nickname that was to stick with John Salmon Ford for the rest of his long life.

John S. Ford was one of the most versatile men to appear in the pages of Texas history. His endeavors ran the gamut from teaching Sunday school to commanding a company of Texas Rangers. A doctor by early training, Ford was also a lawyer, journalist, editor, surveyor, explorer, soldier, public servant, legislator, and historian. He could well be called one of the truly outstanding Texans of his time. Although lacking the sectional and national stature of Sam Houston and John H. Reagan, Ford was closely associated with most of the important events and movements that took place in Texas from his immigration to the Lone Star State in 1836 until his death in 1897. In several of these happenings—the pacification of the Indian frontier during early statehood, blazing a trail from San Antonio to El Paso, the Cortina War, the secession movement, and the Civil War, he played a leading role.

Ford was born in Greenville District, South Carolina, on May 26, 1815. His male forebears on both sides were Virginians and had fought in the American Revolution. In 1817, joining the westward movement, the Ford family migrated to Lincoln County in southern Tennessee where

John's father, William Ford, acquired enough land to be termed a "plantation" owner. According to John Ford's "Memoirs," during his boyhood he "exhibited some marked and rather positive traits of character. He possessed the capacity to get into fights with the boys, to fall in love with the girls, and to take a hand in the deviltry set on foot by his playmates." Thus, at an early age (and by his own admission) Ford developed and displayed the dominant characteristics that would mark his later career—pugnacity, romance, and daring.

Young Ford was not interested in pursuing the hum-drum life of a small planter. He was an avid reader and desired an education. Ford attended the local one-room log schoolhouse and completed the school's rather modest eight-year curriculum in five years. As a promise to his mother he read the Bible daily, and, like Abraham Lincoln, so great was his thirst for knowledge that he borrowed books from his teacher and neighbors until he had exhausted nearby private library sources. Although John Ford's grammar school education qualified him to teach in the rural school system, and he gave this some thought, he sought a greater challenge and turned to the study of medicine.

James G. Barksdale, a well-known Tennessee doctor resided at Shelbyville in Bedford County, just a few miles north of the Ford farm. At the age of nineteen John started his medical study by "reading medicine" under the prominent physician. This was the usual on-the-job training procedure accorded aspiring doctors of the day—medical schools were few in the United States and almost non-existent west of the Alleghenies. Dr. Barksdale found the "interne" courageous as well as an apt trainee. The budding physician gained some local fame by nursing back to health a close acquaintance who had taken smallpox. Ford, fully aware of the contagious aspect of the deadly disease, remained with his sick friend day and night administering to him until he had fully recovered.

In the midst of his medical training John S. Ford heeded the cry of Texas for aid against the incursions of the Mexican dictator, Antonio Lopez de Santa Anna. The young medical student had prepared to leave for the Lone Star State in the spring of 1836, but after the overwhelming Texas victory at San Jacinto he delayed his departure until early summer. Crossing the Sabine in late July, twenty-one-year-old Doctor Ford (as he now called himself) unloaded his belongings in San Augustine. In this East Texas town Ford first hung out his shingle. He would engage in the practice of medicine intermittently for the next sixteen years.

Ford was very active in community affairs during the nine years that he remained in San Augustine. Besides teaching a boys' Sunday school class, and doing some surveying, he organized a local theater group for which he wrote two well-received plays. The versatile doctor was also active in local military affairs, serving at least twice in militia companies organized to combat the Indian menace. It was during this military service that he first met Jack Hays. Ford would later serve with distinction in Hays' Regiment during the Mexican War.

Although Ford's medical practice kept him extremely busy he found time to study law. He passed the East Texas bar in the early 1840's and thus added another shingle to the post in front of his office. Ford's interest in politics had prompted him to take up the study of law and it is doubtful if he ever practiced the profession with much regularity. However, he did dabble in politics while at San Augustine. In the summer of 1840 Ford threw his hat in the ring for one of the two representative seats allotted to San Augustine County. He finished third best, the two seats going to H. W. Augustine and Sam Houston. The following year Ford was again defeated for a seat in the House of Representatives of the Republic and the loss was so convincing that he remained out of politics for several years. He resumed his medical practice full time in 1841 and business was so lucrative that he built a new office closer to the middle of town and acquired a partner, a Dr. Lister. No mere "pill-pusher," Ford performed at least one successful brain operation during his return to full-time medical practice in the early 1840's.

Ford again entered the political arena in the summer of 1844. He stumped the county for representative on a platform that called for the annexation of Texas to the Federal Union and greater protection along the northwestern frontier of the Republic. This time the ambitious physician was successful, polling the most votes of the three candidates involved. Ford was on hand when the Ninth Congress convened at Washington-on-the-Brazos in early December, 1844. He served on a half-dozen important committees, aligned himself with the Houston minority in the House on several issues and introduced the resolution for Texas to join the Federal Union. Favorable action was taken on Ford's resolution, which, coupled with favorable action taken by the Congress of the United States, prepared the way for Texas to become the twenty-seventh star to join the Federal constellation.

In late 1845, following his term in the House, the lawyer-physician decided to give up medicine and engage in the newspaper business. During the Texas Constitutional Convention of July, 1845 (a necessary step to statehood), Ford had served as the official correspondent of the *Texas National Register*, a newspaper published at Washington-on-the-Brazos. This short stint at journalism whetted Ford's appetite for the newspaper business, and, in partnership with Mike Cronicon, he purchased the *Register* and moved it to Austin. Thus commenced Ford's fascination for journalism, a field in which he retained an interest for most of his life. Under the able direction of Ford and Cronicon, the *Texas National Register* (later the *Texas Democrat*) became one of the outstanding early newspapers of Texas. The weekly was decidedly pro-Houston and for a while its existence was jeopardized—Austin was a town where the old general was despised and ridiculed. However, by March of 1845, the liberal Democratic organ was publishing semi-weekly and the following month Ford and Cronicon were elected state printers—quite a plum for the new publishing team. John S. Ford's first venture into the newspaper business was most successful.

When Ford's second wife (his first marriage in Tennessee when he was nineteen ended in divorce) became seriously ill in the summer of 1845, he left the management of the paper to Mike Cronicon and spent all of his time administering to his ailing mate. Her death in early August, 1845, caused Ford to isolate himself from the outside world for many weeks. He lost interest in his profession, in politics, and in his newspaper. After emerging from his period of sorrow, Ford turned his back on his old pursuits and threw his boundless energy into a new challenge—the profession of arms. The United States had declared war against Mexico on May 12, 1846 and Texas had been called upon to furnish her quota of troops. This is the distraction that Ford sought in which to bury his sorrow. At thirty-one he would embark upon a career in which he was to gain his greatest success and make his mark in Texas history. As a soldier in the Mexican and Civil wars and as a Texas Ranger between wars John S. Ford would reach the pinnacle of his fame.

Ford followed with great interest the exploits of Colonel Jack Hays' Regiment of Rangers assigned to Zachary Taylor's command. The Rangers, instrumental in the early victories of Taylor's army along the Rio Grande and at Monterrey, had excited the imagination of the Texans, including the doctor-publisher, who had met the dynamic Hays while both were engaged in protecting the frontier in the late 1830's. Ford could not resist the call issued by Hays in the spring of 1847 to augment his force, and thus enlisted as a private in the Ranger Regiment on May 10. He was soon promoted to lieutenant and was transferred to Hays' staff as the regimental adjutant—a position that he would occupy, except for short periods of time, until the end of the war. Serving with Jack Hays in the Mexican War was one of the high points of Ford's long career as a public servant.

In the summer of 1847 Colonel Hays' Regiment was transferred from

Taylor's jurisdiction to that of Winfield Scott who commanded the American army advancing on Mexico City from Vera Cruz. During August the Ranger regiment (officially known as the First Regiment of Texas Mounted Volunteers) marched for the Gulf Coast via Mier and embarked at Brazos Santiago for Vera Cruz. The voyage to Mexico was uneventful for Adjutant Ford except for the behavior of his horse, "Old Higgins," a nasty but fast mount that had been assigned to Ford when he had enlisted in the Rangers at San Antonio. It appears that an arrogant Irish seaman who had gone out of his way to heckle the Rangers, met more than his match when he took to teasing the horses of the Texans. As the trouble maker approched Old Higgins, the perverse beast reached out and with his powerful jaws and teeth cleanly severed Paddy's ear from his head, and then calmly proceeded to chew up the appendage and swallow it. The howling Hibernian did not molest the Texans or their horses for the rest of the voyage.

For several weeks after landing in Mexico the Rangers encamped near Vera Cruz, Scott's major supply base for his Mexico City campaign. During this period Hays' regiment was primarily engaged in protecting the eastern end of Scott's supply line against the raids of Mexican guerrillas led by Padre Jarauta and by Zenobia. Many sharp encounters between the Mexican irregulars and Hays' Rangers took place, Ford taking part in several of them and leading the Rangers in at least one attack. It was while the Texans were operating near Vera Cruz, that Lieutenant Ford received permission to form a spy company. Ford was elected captain of the company which was comprised of a half-hundred picked Rangers noted for their marksmanship and scouting ability. Its purpose was to raid the nearby hills and villages seeking out and destroying bandits and guerrillas. Although the spy company performed well, it was disbanded in late October when Hays' Regiment was ordered to join General Scott at Mexico City.

Soon after the Rangers had landed in Mexico they were introduced to the intricacies of the Colt six-shooter, a gun that they would make famous and, in turn, would make them famous. Colt's revolver was an enigma for several of the Texans. Some of the pistols exploded when the Rangers jammed the conical bullets in backward. On a few occasions when re-loading, powder was spilled around the revolving cylinder exploding all six shots at once when the gun was fired. Ford in his "Memoirs" recorded an instance where he found a recruit cleaning his six-shooter while it was fully loaded and still retained the percussion caps on the cylinder. After admonishing the young Ranger for his carelessness Ford passed on. In a few minutes Rip heard a loud report from the soldier's tent. Hastening back to the vicinity of the noise he found that the recruit had accidentally shot his own horse through the head.

Hays' Rangers rode with General Robert Patterson's column on the march to join Scott and had to fight off Mexican guerrillas during the entire 260-mile trip to the capital city. Ford was plagued with yellow fever during much of the trek inland, and this limited somewhat his participation in the forays against Jarauta's and Zenobia's irregulars that constantly stung the flanks and rear of the American force.

The Rangers reached the environs of Mexico City on December 7, 1847. Hays' mounted volunteers presented quite a sight as they joined Scott's army of occupation garrisoning the walled city. A war correspondent present reported that Hays' Regiment wore non-descript clothing shredded by constant campaigning. Some soldiers, he wrote, had appropriated articles of local color from serapes to sombrerors; a few had retained the broad-brimmed Texas hats and at least one man wore a high silk hat. It appeared, however, that the majority of the Rangers wore a headgear with a tail hanging from it—skins of dogs, cats, bears, coons, and wildcats being the most prevalent hat material. They rode into the capital in route order—many straggled, and while most of the Rangers rode in the orthodox fashion, a few rode into town sideways, standing in the saddle, and even facing to the rear. It was a sight that Scott's regulars and the Mexican onlookers could and would not easily forget.

During the American occupation of the capital a group of Mexican thieves and murderers, known as *léperos* inhabited the streets of the city. These plug-uglies struck fear into the hearts of the civilians and terrorized soldiers who wandered from the confines of their billets. The *léperos* had the population cowered until "Los Diablos Tejanos" (the Texas Devils) or "los Tejanos san grientos" (the bloody Texans), as Hays' Rangers were tabbed by the Mexicans, rode into town. Asking no quarter and giving none, the Texans immediately clashed with the ruffians whose primary weapons consisted of cobble stones and knives—no match for the fast-firing Colts. After several confrontations with the Rangers, one in which eighty of the scoundrels were killed, the *lépero* gangs were broken up and the survivors melted into the peaceful element of the population.

Following the signing of the Treaty of Guadalupe Hidalgo on February 2, 1848, Hays' regiment, including Adjutant John S. Ford, left Mexico City and rode for the coast. Near Vera Cruz in early May the regiment of Rangers, except for Hays and Ford, was mustered out of the Federal army. Mexican War service would mark the only time that the Texas Rangers would serve as a unit in the United States armed forces during a major conflict. Colonel Hays and Rip Ford, intending to join the Frontier Battalion of Rangers in Texas, disembarked at Port Lavaca about May 10, where they were greeted as national heroes. Their success in leading *Los Diablos Tejanos* against the Mexican renegades and irregulars had excited the imagination of the Texas people who were still rankled by Mexican atrocities committed during the Texas War and the years following.

Sometime during the voyage from Vera Cruz to Texas, Ford apparently decided to leave the Rangers and thus was mustered out of the service on May 14, 1848. He returned to Austin shortly thereafter and resumed his editorship of the *Texas Democrat*. This ended Ford's first period of service as a Texas Ranger. He had performed well as a Ranger and was commended for his service in the Mexican War by General "Old Gritter Face" Joe Lane, to whose brigade Hays' regiment had been attached. Too, Adjutant Ford had learned much from Jack Hays, a man he greatly admired and whom he sought to emulate in his future service with the famous Texas law enforcement agency and guardians of the frontier.

Between the Mexican and the Civil War Rip Ford was active in state affairs and reached the zenith of his Ranger career. Tiring of the newspaper business in late 1848, he sold his interest in the *Democrat* and sought permission from the state to raise a volunteer company of Rangers to patrol the northwestern frontier. Ford, denied this opportunity because of a shortage of state funds, retired to his Austin home and became an avid reader of military history and tactics—the Mexican War and Ranger service had whetted his appetite for a military career. Largely forsaking his other professions, the doctor would devote the greater part of the next fifteen years to the profession of arms.

Ford laid aside his books on military science long enough in early 1849 to make a very worthwhile contribution to the state and the nation. In concert with Indian Agent Robert Simpson Neighbors, he helped to blaze a trail from San Antonio to El Paso. When the California gold fever hit the United States tens of thousands of Americans converged on the Golden State. Several routes were used to reach the gold fields— around the Horn, across the Isthmus of Panama and Nicaragua, and cross-country from the Mississippi Valley to the Pacific Coast. Hoping to persuade Southern gold enthusiasts to approach California through the Lone Star State, Texas businessmen sought a practical route through the state to California by the way of El Paso. Neighbors, who was about to embark on a trip to El Paso for the U. S. Army, agreed to have the ex-Ranger join him on the trek.

Neighbors, leaving San Antonio, headquarters for the Military District of Texas, in late February, 1849 was joined by Ford at Austin and together the two trail blazers rode north toward Waco. From the vicinity of Waco, the Indian agent and doctor, accompanied by a respectable entourage of white men and friendly Indians, rode west toward El Paso. The journey through West Texas was without incident and the Neighbors-Ford party covered the round-trip from San Antonio to El Paso, almost 1,200 miles, in fifty-five days. Ford kept a detailed account of the trip and upon his return to Austin in June, published a lengthy report of the expedition. Not only did his account specify clearly the most practicable wagon route to El Paso but included, as well, a proposal for a railroad route along the thirty-second parallel. Within a few months after Ford's return, a wagon train following the same path, proved the practicability of the route by making the journey from El Paso to Austin in twenty-three days. The Ford-Neighbors Trail proved highly successful and continued to be the main pathway through West Texas until replaced by the iron horse.

The trip to El Paso enabled Ford to meet one of the real characters of that West Texas community—a powerful bit of "femininity" known as "Great Western." Great Western was a huge, well-built woman who operated a combination hotel and gambling emporium in the border town. She was reported to have been able to out-fight, out-shoot, and out-gamble any man in the area. According to legend, Great Western had fallen in love with General Zachary Taylor while they were both in Florida. When the Mexican War started and Taylor moved to the Rio Grande, she came to El Paso and purchased a hotel. It was reported that shortly after the battle of Buena Vista when a participant in that engagement came into El Paso and announced Taylor's defeat the hefty hotel keeper picked up the bearer of bad tidings and roared in his ear, "You damned [s.o.b.] there ain't Mexicans enough in Mexico to whip old Taylor." Great Western supposedly remained true to "Old Rough and Ready" the rest of her life.

During the winter of 1848-49, the settlers between the Nueces and Rio Grande rivers were victimized by an increase in the tempo of Comanche and Mexican bandit raids. General G. M. Brooke, commander of the Texas Military District, unable to cope with the situation because of the paucity of United States troops in the area, authorized the formation of three Ranger companies at Federal expense to help stem the depredations. Rip Ford, whose qualifications as a soldier and whose eagerness to return to Ranger service were well-known, was given permission to raise one of the three companies. Ford's company of some seventy-five men was mustered into the Federal service in late August, 1849 and assigned to duty station just south of Corpus Christi. Most of the men in the company had seen service with Jack Hays' Regiment in the Mexican War and as a lot they were unruly and heavy drinkers but expert fighters. However, Ford, one of the few Ranger officers of that day who believed in discipline and drill, soon had his contingent of frontiersmen whipped into a well-organized fighting unit. While the United States Government provided percussion rifles, pistols, holsters and ammunition, each Ranger had to furnish his own horse, saddle, bridle, halter and lariat. For his logistical support and service, the Ranger was paid $23.50 monthly.

Ford's company, which was originally mustered for only six months, was re-enlisted on three occasions and thus spent two years in the Federal service. While Rip's command saw little action against Mexican border bandits it did skirmish a great deal with the Comanches. The climax of the Indian fighting came with the Amargosa affair which occurred on May 12, 1850 along the banks of the Nueces. Although the action involved only about a dozen and a half men on each side it was a bitter, hand-to-hand battle which the Rangers finally won, killing or wounding all but two of the Comanches. Ford, during the action, was grazed by an arrow across the back of his right hand. Although the wound was slight, the arrow apparently had been dipped in rattlesnake venom for the Ranger captain had only partial use of his arm for the next several years. The use of his left arm was not the only loss that Ford suffered during the Comanche campaigns of 1850—his famous mount, Old Higgins, was stolen by a Comanche raid in August. In later years the physician-soldier often wondered how many one-eared Comanches were roaming the plains of West Texas, victims of the cantankerous mount with the strong jaws and sharp teeth.

"Ford's Old Company," as his 1849-51 Ranger contingent was known, was mustered out of Federal service at Laredo on September 23, 1851. The Rangers under Ford's energetic command had cleared the area between the Nueces and the Rio Grande of hostile Indians and their presence alone had discouraged forays by Mexican renegades. Ford, however, after the company was disbanded became personally involved in Mexican political affairs. He sought to help his old friend, Texas-born, Virginia-educated Jose M. J. Carbajal set up an independent and democratic republic along the Rio Grande. The attempt at nationhood was unsuccessful and Ford and Carbajal barely escaped to Texas one jump ahead of the Mexican National Army. Rip Ford was criticized in some circles for dabbling in Mexican affairs but he defended his participation by proclaiming that he was helping people who were "resisting tyranny" and "battling for the exercise of their privileges as free men."

In January, 1852, following his two-year hitch with the Rangers and ill-conceived participation in Carbajal's "El Plan de la Loba," Ford returned to Austin. For the next six years he would divide his time between politics and publishing. On January 12, Ford was elected state senator to fill the vacancy created by the death of Ed Burleson. Before the ex-Ranger left office—on the last day of the session, he gave an impassioned speech on the poor state of frontier defense. Within a few years Ford would take an active part in correcting this situation and enhance his reputation as one of the outstanding Rangers of the early period.

After filling Burleson's unexpired term, Ford remained at Austin and once again was attracted by the smell of printer's ink. He bought the *South-Western American* in November, 1852 and immediately espoused a series of causes including the support of slavery, a state-backed railroad, and the temperance movement. Editor Ford also drummed for a permanent Ranger service—a cause that was dear to his heart, and weekly damned the new Republican Party as an un-American institution. Ford proved to be an able editor and writer and was deemed a worthy competitor by the publishers of the *Texas State Gazette* with whom he engaged in a friendly rivalry.

Rip, as interested in local politics as he was the state political scene, in December, 1853 was elected mayor of the capital city. His administration was highlighted by several temperance actions, the principal one of which prohibited the sale of liquor on Sundays. Although not affiliated with any particular church, Ford was an avowed prohibitionist. On one occasion during his term of office he fired the town marshal for being drunk and assumed the position of keeping law and order up and down Congress Avenue himself. Although Mayor Ford did not engage in a gunfight during his wearing of the star, he is supposed to have stared down at least one inebriated gunslinger. The pistol-wielding trouble-maker is said to have fled the city when he learned that the law enforcement officer confronting him was the old Ranger, Rip Ford.

After a year's sojourn at city hall, Ford returned to the newspaper business. He changed the name of his paper from the *South-Western American* to the *Texas State Times* and proclaimed on the new masthead that it was the largest weekly in Texas with the exception of the Galveston *News*. Soon after his stint as mayor, Ford became disenchanted with the Democratic Party and enchanted with the Know-Nothing or Native American Party—an anti-Catholic, anti-foreign, and anti-Semetic rightest organization. In fact Ford's paper became the official organ of the party in Texas and 'Old Rip" rose to a prominent position with the state organization, serving as chairman on two important committees.

The ex-mayor of Austin drifted still more to the right during the mid-1850's when he organized the Order of the Lone Star of the West, a forerunner of the Knights of the Golden Circle—the secessionist agitators who helped to push Texas out of the Union. The primary purpose of the Order of the Lone Star, a secret, mystic organization, was to set up a slave empire with headquarters at Havana. The dream of the slave empire never materialized and by late 1856 Ford had come to his senses. He disbanded the Order of the Lone Star of the West, lost interest in the Know-Nothing movement, and returned to the folds of the Democratic Party. The Democratic victory in 1856 killed the Know-Nothing Party movement in Texas and the Knights of the Golden Circle, a sectional rather than a state pro-slavery movement, took over the remnants of Ford's pro-slavery Texas organization.

Ford, tired of politics and disgusted by public criticism of his flirtation with the right, suspended operations of the *Texas State Times* in June, 1857 and sold the paper the following August. He then withdrew from capital journalism and embarked on an extended sight-seeing tour of the Lone Star State. While traveling along the frontier he witnessed first-hand the results of the Comanche raids and now more than ever he was convinced that some dramatic steps had to be taken to safeguard the fringe settlements. Ford would soon have the opportunity of turning his convictions into action and would play a leading role in not only pacifying the frontier but also of safeguarding the border along the Rio Grande.

The years 1858 and 1859 in Texas were tailor-made for action, Rip Ford style. The Comanches, notwithstanding the presence of the famed 2nd U. S. Cavalry, were causing havoc along the northern and western frontiers and Juan Cortina, the self-styled "Robin Hood of Mexico," was terrorizing the lower Rio Grande. There was more fighting in Texas during these two years than any time since the Revolutionary War year of 1836.

Hardin R. Runnels, victor for governor in 1857 over Sam Houston, determined to beef-up the frontier defense force. The passage of "an act for the better protection of the frontier" by the legislature in late January, 1858, enabled the governor to augment the state defense forces by a full Ranger company. Runnels immediately appointed John S. Ford to the rank of major and senior captain of the Rangers and gave him command jurisdiction over the few small minute and Ranger companies then in the field. According to the late biographer of the Rangers, Dr. Walter P. Webb, "The governor's choice of Ford as supreme commander was a wise one. In fact, no better man could have been found in Texas to execute such bold designs as were now on foot." Ford's orders from the state executive were to seek out and attack the Comanche in his heartland above the Red River and to deal him a blow from which he would be a long time recovering. This would have been an impossible order to execute for a man of lesser talent and fighting ability than that possessed by Rip Ford. The senior Ranger captain carried out the governor's bold designs well-nigh to perfection.

Major Ford's command left Austin on a chilly February morning in 1858 and proceeded in four parallel columns along the frontier from Brown County north to the Brazos Indian Reservation. The men, besides being expertly led, were well-mounted, and well-armed—the Rangers carried enough hand guns and shoulder arms to fire 1,500 rounds without reloading. The Comanches were in for trouble!

To augment this one hundred-man Ranger force, Ford requested Shapley P. Ross, well-known Indian fighter and agent, to raise one hundred friendly Indians from the Brazos Reservation. This Ross proceeded to do and the two columns finally joined forces at Cottonwood Springs (Young County) early on April 26, 1858. Scouts had brought back word that the main body of the Comanches was camped along the Canadian River near Antelope Hills in what is now the state of Oklahoma. Under the overall jurisdiction of Rip Ford the dual command prepared to move into the lair of the Redman, 150 miles to the north.

The Ford-Ross column actually got under way late on April 26. Three days later the two hundred-plus man force (including Ford's seventy-three-year-old father who had joined his son in the field in mid-April) crossed the Red River into the Indian Territory. The Texans proceeded west along the north bank of the river—scouts to the front and flank looking for signs of the Comanche. On May 7, the column marched north from the Red River for the Washita; a branch of this stream was reached the following day. The Rangers were now approaching the Comanche heartland and both speed and surprise were essential for a successful campaign. The column picked up the tempo of their advance, marching night and day on May 9 and 10. On May 11 a few Comanche riders were seen at a distance and scouts sighted a small outlying village a few miles ahead of the Texans and their Indian allies. In a parley between Ford and Ross it was decided that they would attack the Indian village in a double-flanking movement early the following day and then push on immediately for the main village thought to be a few miles beyond. All was in readiness now to spring the trap on the unsuspecting Comanche in his own backyard.

Ford at this stage of his career was forty-three years old, lithe, erect, and of medium stature. He had curly light-brown hair speckled with gray, blue eyes, high cheek bones, and an aquiline nose. He was ordinarily soft-spoken but occasionally resorted to profanity in the heat of battle. The Ranger captain was a tee-totaler and read a passage from the Bible daily, even when campaigning—fulfilling two promises that he had made to his mother when a young man. Ford had few if any peers with a six-shooter. It was said that he could hit a man every time with a Colt at 125 yards. He required but a few hours' sleep and had the habit of giving each man in his command a nickname. In the same vein his men invariably referred to him as "Old Rip." This was the man who was to lead a Ranger company in what was to be the largest and most famous Indian battle in Ranger history.

Early on the morning of May 12, the Texas invaders advanced, Ross and the Reservation Indians on the right, Ford and the Rangers on the left. Out of the hills they moved and down toward the valley of the Canadian River. After advancing about six miles—the time 7 a.m., the five Indian lodges sighted the previous day came into view. To the din of Texas yells and Indian warwhoops, Ford and Ross charged toward the lodges, capturing and killing several braves and taking numerous horses. Unfortunately, two Comanches mounted their ponies and were able to escape the tide of Texans that overran the small village. Ford immediately gave the order to continue the advance and the two columns (except for the friendly Tonkawas who had stopped to loot the village and procure horses) rode north at a rapid pace toward the main village. Upon approaching the crest of a slight rise, Captain Ford saw the numerous white lodges of the Tenawa Comanches glittering in the sun some three miles distant on the north bank of the Canadian. Ranger scouts estimated the village to house some 350 warriors. The men were ordered forward—Ford and Ross had found their quarry and now moved in for the kill.

Across the shallow but broad Canadian the Rangers and friendly Indians swarmed. The Comanches, even though alerted by the two escaping braves, had elected to make a stand at their village rather than at the river bank, although the latter would have been more feasible from a tactical standpoint. The reason for the Comanche stand at their village became apparent as the Texans drew closer. As Ford and Ross approached within 200 yards of the mass of lodges, now seething with painted Comanches, a solitary figure on a magnificent horse rode out to meet them. It was Pohebits Quasho or Iron Jacket, head chief of the village. The chief was wearing powerful medicine, a coat of scaled mail that extended from his throat to his thighs, a tunic of armor probably appropriated from a Spanish conquistador by an ancestor. Iron Jacket claimed that when wearing his extended jerkin of metal he and his warriors were invincible. The test of this invincibility had now come.

The armored chief, putting his charger through a series of short circles, holding his rifle aloft, and with menacing facial contortions, eased toward the Rangers and their Indian allies, who had halted momentarily, transfixed by the weird ceremony unfolding before them. The stillness was suddenly shattered by Ranger Lieutenant Billy Pitts who bellowed out, "Kill the [s.o.b.]." Instantly several shots rang out and the chief's horse crashed to the ground. Iron Jacket, still clutching his rifle, fell free of his mount. Staggering toward his attackers, he brought the rifle to his shoulder but before he could fire he was cut down by a concentrated volley. Twisting grotesquely, the Comanche chief crumpled to the ground, a mass of blood, feathers, and metal. A shot in the head at close range finished him.

The Comanche warriors, flustered and upset by the demise of their chief and the failure of his protective medicine, milled around in consternation looking for leadership. Ford, sensing the situation, immediately ordered his yelling Rangers to close on the Comanches. Ross did likewise and a battle royal ensued over an area estimated at six miles long and three miles in width along the north bank of the Canadian. Fighting in small groups and as individuals the Rangers and friendly Indians (identified by a patch of white cloth tied to their headdress) engaged the Comanches. Slowly but surely Iron Jacket's followers were pushed through the village across the prairie and into the foothills beyond. The cries of the wounded and the screams of the women and children rose above the din of battle. Knives, tomahawks, lances, and arrows were no match for the carbines and the six-shooters. "Captain Ford," Ranger Sergeant Bob Cotter reported, ". . . was everywhere, directing and controlling the movement of his men." Finally, when the sun was directly overhead and the mounts were jaded and the men exhausted, the Rangers and their Indian allies broke off the engagement and returned to the village.

The victory over the Tenawa Comanches was complete. As Ford and his men rode back through the shattered lodges they noted the scattered debris and aftermath of battle. Iron Jacket's naked form lay sprawled in the dust. Rangers and friendly Indians had pulled the mail shingles from his armor in a manner reminiscent of housewives plucking feathers from a chicken. Many of the Comanche dead had their hands and feet cut off. Ford noted that the missing extremities were dangling from the saddles of the Tonkawas—they would serve as the *piece de resistance* for the cannibalistic Tonks' victory feast that night over their old enemies. By nightfall on the twelfth, Ford and his command were camped some twelve miles south of the Canadian, and while the Rangers rested, the Tonks nibbled on their grisly fare. An assessment of losses for the Rangers revealed two killed and two badly wounded out of the 102 engaged. The Texans in turn had killed seventy-six Comanches, captured over 300 horses, and had in tow eighteen prisoners. The rest of Iron Jacket's band, including scores of wounded, had been scattered.

Captain Ford made his way back into Texas at a leisurely pace. By May 12 he had reached Camp Runnels, a few miles north of present-day Breckenridge, the site from which he had started his march north in late April. The successful Canadian River campaign was conducted over a thirty-day period. It proved that the Comanches could be beaten in their own territory provided that the leadership was both aggressive and courageous. John S. Ford had provided that. He had marched some 500 miles, much of it in unfamiliar territory, had fought a six-hour battle, and had led his striking force safely back from the enemy's heartland.

A few months after the Ford-Ross victory on the upper Indian frontier, Captain Earl Van Dorn of the 2nd U. S. Cavalry repeated the trick with almost as much success. Van Dorn with five companies of regulars accompanied by L. S. "Sul" Ross, son of Shapley, with 125 Reservation Indians struck the Comanches a stunning blow on October 1, 1858. From his base on Otter Creek in Indian Territory, the cavalryman marched ninety miles east in thirty-seven hours. He surprised a village of over one hundred and twenty lodges and in a bitter hand-to-hand battle, similar to the Ford-Ross engagement, killed fifty-six Indian warriors. Van Dorn burned all of the lodges, captured 300 horses, and drove the surviving Indians into the mountains. Five regulars were killed, including two officers, and eight others were wounded, including Earl Van Dorn and Ross.

Rip Ford's next Ranger spectacular and contribution to the security of his state was his participation in the so-called Cortina War in 1859-60. Juan Cortina, a Mexican national with more than ordinary military ability, posing as the protector of down-trodden Mexican-Americans, raided and captured Brownsville in late September, 1859. Cortina held the city for several days then moved outside, cutting off land communications to and from the beleaguered Texas town during October and November. A small company of Rangers under Captain W. G. Tobin was the first outside help to reach Brownsville. Tobin's company, which did not measure up to the usual Ranger standards, and a local militia unit, the "Brownsville Tigers," attacked Cortina and were badly defeated. The Mexican leader now became more brazen than ever—he flew the Mexican flag on American territory and openly recruited Mexican-Americans for his army. Finally in December, United States regulars under the command of Major Samuel P. Heintzelman were sent south to subdue the pesky Cortina and his followers.

Ford had seen little Ranger service since his Canadian River campaign. He had organized and commanded a six-months company during the winter of 1858-59 but when Cortina struck Brownsville in September he was at Austin nursing a siege of malaria. At Governor Runnels' request, he organized a Ranger company in November, 1858 for the express purpose of bringing the Mexican to bay. The governor designated Rip's rank as that of major and placed him in command of all state forces operating on the Rio Grande. Major Ford proceeded south from Austin gathering recruits as he approached the border. He arrived with fifty-three men at Brownsville on December 14, just a few hours too late to assist Major Heintzelman and Captain Tobin defeat Cortina at the battle of La Ebronal.

The story of the Cortina War from the time of the fight at La Ebronal on December 14 to the final scattering of the Mexican forces in March, 1860 is one of continual victory for the American forces. Except for the first engagement at La Ebronal, Major Ford and his company played a key role in the defeat and dispersion of the "Mexican Robin Hood" and his men. Following the victory on December 14, Heintzelman and Ford (operating under Heintzelman's orders) followed the Mexican "general" up the river past Barstone and Edinburg to Rio Grande City. Here, Cortina had established a defense line bolstered by two artillery pieces that he had captured earlier from the Brownsville militia. Ford opened the fighting at Rio Grande City, routing the enemy before Heintzelman's regulars could come up. The Rangers pursued the Mexicans up the Roma road, driving Cortina and most of his command into Mexico and capturing his two artillery pieces. Ford was at his best at Rio Grande City—he personally led a charge against the Mexican artillery, narrowly missing decapitation by a charge of grapeshot, and then successfully led his men against a Mexican roadblock on the Roma road. The battle of Rio Grande City on December 27 was a Ranger victory all the way—Heintzelman's forces played but a small role.

After the debacle on December 27, Cortina remained in Mexico reorganizing and recruiting for his shattered forces. By early February,

1860 he had fortified a bend in the Rio Grande called La Bolsa, some thirty-five miles north of Brownsville, and attempted to control river traffic. His primary objective was the steamer *Ranchero,* a river boat carrying goods and specie valued at $200,000 to Brownsville. Ford's company was designated as the military escort for the ship as it steamed down the Rio Grande in early February. As the vessel came within range of Cortina's guns on February 4 he opened fire, bringing the Rangers up fast. Ferried to the south side of the river by the *Ranchero,* Ford and less than fifty Rangers attacked the strong Mexican position at La Bolsa. Rip in his haste to get across the river and close with the enemy had left his personal weapons on the American side. With borrowed guns he led a charge against Cortina's foot soldiers, while a dozen of his men with rifles kept the Mexican horsemen at a distance. Cortina's left flank, protected by a palisade fence, collapsed under the deadly fire of the Rangers' six-shooters. His center then panicked and the entire force of 300 stampeded toward the chapparal and safety. Cortina was the last to leave the field; acting as the solitary rear guard until his men had disappeared in the brush, he miraculously rode away unscathed. La Bolsa was one of Ford's greatest Ranger victories. Cortina's losses were twenty-nine killed and forty wounded; the Ranger losses amounted to one killed and four wounded.

Juan Cortina, although he had been soundly beaten at La Ebronal, Rio Grande City, and La Bolsa, still posed a threat to American settlements along the Rio Grande. Major Ford's Rangers and two companies of Federal cavalry under Captain George Stoneman continued to patrol the river and search for Señor Juan and his men until late March. Only one engagement between the Mexican leader and the Americans took place during this closing phase of the abbreviated Cortina War. Crossing to the Mexican side of the river on March 18, Ford and Stoneman surprised the Mexicans at La Mesa, rolled up both flanks and captured all but a handful of men. Cortina, as elusive as the famed Scarlet Pimpernal, escaped again and fled toward rancho Maguey, sixty miles south of Matamoras. Riding deep into Mexico, Ford and Stoneman pursued the wily bandit leader to Maguey, only to find he had fled toward Monterrey. They continued the pursuit for some forty more miles but the weariness of their horses and lack of food and forage forced the Rangers and cavalrymen to return to the north side of the Rio Grande on March 21.

By April, 1860 the Cortina War was over. Cortina went into hiding deep in Mexico, his followers deserted in wholesale lots, and Mexican border officials withdrew their support of him. The war had cost the United States one-third of a million dollars in property loss alone and had taken the lives of ninety-five Americans and friendly Mexicans. Cortina is estimated to have had 150 men killed and several hundred wounded. The war had enhanced Ford's stature as an aggressive Ranger leader and his name, once again, became a household word in Texas. He and his Rangers had practically single-handed won the two major battles of the war, Rio Grande City and La Bolsa, and had shared honors with George Stoneman at La Mesa. Thanks to Samuel Stone Hall's dime novels published by Beadle's New York Library, "Old Rip's" exploits during the Cortina War were embellished upon and in the 1870's and '80's he became a national hero to the tens of thousands of young readers of Beadle's books.

In early April, 1860 Lieutenant-Colonel Robert E. Lee, acting commander of the Texas Military District, inspected the scenes of the Cortina War. Ford had supper with the famous officer on the evening of April 7 at Edinburg, and was quite impressed with the cavalry colonel whom he found to be a "man of superior intellect, possessing the capacity to accomplish great ends, and the gift of controlling and leading men." Rip Ford was not only a great leader himself but apparently had the knack of recognizing leadership ability in others.

In mid-May, 1860, at Goliad, the Ranger companies that had been organized in late 1859 to combat Juan Cortina were mustered out. Ford was discharged with the other officers and thus came to a close his colorful and useful career as a Texas Ranger. He had made a great contribution to the state during his long service dating from the Mexican War. Authorities on the Rangers rank him with Jack Hays, Bigfoot Wallace, Ben McCulloch, and Samuel H. Walker as the greatest Rangers of the pre-Civil War era. He upheld and contributed to the great tradition of the Texas Rangers—a tradition that has made that service the greatest law enforcement agency in history.

However, the spring of 1860 did not mark the end of John S. Ford's contribution to his state nor see the lessening of his public responsibilities. He was to play a major role in the secession movement in Texas and the Civil War and reconstruction era that followed.

After the election of Abraham Lincoln in November, 1860, Austin boiled with excitement and unrest as the ultra-secessionists and Unionists vied for public support. Ford immediately declared for the state righters and was very active in swaying public opinion in Travis County for the South. He was one of the prime movers in calling the secession convention on January 28, 1861, and served as a delegate from Cameron County to the convention. The ex-major of the Rangers was active at the convention. He helped to elect Oran M. Roberts president and worked with the committee that drew up the Ordinance of Secession—the document that took Texas out of the Union.

On March 3 Rip Ford, Henry E. McCulloch, and Henry's brother Ben were commissioned as colonels in the cavalry of the state forces. These appointments were made by the Committee on Public Safety who then ordered the three commanders to seize the U.S. military posts in Texas. Ford's area of operation and responsibility was the Rio Grande Valley, a logical choice since he had campaigned through much of that region during the Cortina War. Colonel Ford successfully carried out his mission. Landing his regiment at Brazos de Santiago, Ford persuaded the commander of Fort Brown to surrender all Federal installations along the river. It was a bloodless effort that netted Texas and the Confederacy a sizeable military plum. The other two Texas commanders had the same success. In all, twenty-one Federal installations were surrendered to the Texans, thus neutralizing fifteen per cent of the regular National Army (2,500 men) and giving the state (and the Confederacy) between two and three million dollars worth of military stores and supplies.

For the next few months Colonel Ford would command the Texas Mounted Rifles, later to be re-designated the 2nd Texas Cavalry Regiment, with duty station along the Rio Grande. His mission was to prevent a Federal invasion by way of Brownsville and to guard the border against Mexican raids. Ford, during his tenure as field commander of Confederate forces on the Rio Grande, negotiated an important trade agreement between the Confederacy and Mexico and kept Mexican border raids to a minimum. In June, 1862, General H. P. Bee, commander of the Military Sub-District of the Rio Grande, appointed Rip superintendent of conscripts with headquarters at Austin. Ford also had the dual responsibility of commanding officer of the Houston conscript camp. The Confederate Conscription Act passed on April 16, 1862 by the Confederate Congress was the first draft law to be enacted in the United States. It required all white male citizens eighteen to thirty-five years of age to enroll for military service. Enrolling officers with the rank of captain in the Confederate Army were designated for each county, and camps of instruction were established in several locations throughout the state to give the conscripts basic training. Although not wholly in favor of the conscription law, Ford continued in the capacity of state superintendent until November, 1862 when he resigned his post and reverted to the status of a private citizen.

When flamboyant General "Prince John" Magruder assumed command of the District of Texas, New Mexico, and Arizona in the newly-created Confederate Department of the Trans-Mississippi, he induced Ford in March, 1863 to re-assume the duty as state superintendent of conscripts. Ford carried out his duties conscientiously and was praised for his fearless and honest application of the difficult conscription laws. However, the ex-Ranger disliked administrative work regardless of its importance and hoped to obtain a field command.

Ford's wish for active service was soon realized thanks to the Federal occupation of the lower Rio Grande by a substantial force under General N. J. T. Dana during November, 1863. Although reluctant to remove Ford from his position as head of the Texas Conscript Bureau, Magruder finally consented under pressure from prominent Rio Grande residents to send him south to counter the Federal invasion. In late December, 1863 General Magruder designated Colonel Ford as commander of all state and Confederate troops assigned south and west of San Antonio. In order to augment his command, Ford was given the authority to raise as many companies as he could among men exempt from conscription. As it turned out, these men, attracted by short terms of enlistment and service within the state, provided the largest contingent of Rip's force. His new command, designated as the Rio Grande Expeditionary Force, would be the largest and in some ways the most important military command of his career.

Ford spent the winter and early spring of 1864 directing the operation of the far-flung units under his jurisdiction, assembling a competent staff for his expeditionary force, and inducing those exempt from conscription to "join up." By mid-April Ford and the greater part of his command were concentrated at Laredo. His expeditionary force which would operate primarily in the lower Rio Grande area from Laredo south to Brownsville (a distance of 200 miles), left Laredo in late April, 1864, driving south along the river for the coast. By the last of July, the Confederates with little effort had driven the Federal forces from the Rio Grande Valley back to their base of operations at Brazos Santiago. Ford, a favorite with the residents of the Valley since his Ranger days there, was hailed as a conquering hero and presented with a silk flag made by the ladies of Brownsville. Rip, exhausted by the summer campaign and falling victim to another malaria attack, was confined to bed for the balance of the summer.

The Federal military force in the Valley, which was restricted to Brazos Island after July, 1864, showed little disposition to challenge Ford's control of the area. Hence, Rip, after his return to duty, was concerned primarily with maintaining good relations with the Mexican and French forces hovering on the south bank of the Rio Grande. With a skill that would have done justice to a trained diplomat, Colonel Ford maneuvered delicately along the fringe of international intrigue and inter-Mexican bickerings that seethed south of the river and that threatened but did not involve his command. Otherwise, the winter and spring of 1865 were seasons of tranquility for Ford and his expeditionary force.

Ironically, the last battle of the Civil War was fought in the obscure corner of the Confederacy where John S. Ford had command. On May 13, 1865, some five weeks after Lee surrendered to Grant at Appomattox Courthouse, Federal forces stationed at Brazos Island engaged Confederate forces under Ford at Palmito Ranch. On May 12, three Federal regiments and a few dismounted Texas Union cavalry companies under the overall command of Colonel T. H. Barrett, attempted to capture Fort Brown. Ford, unaware of Lee's surrender and alerted to the Federal movement, hastily brought up his artillery and cavalry to support his infantry. In a running fight on the afternoon of May 13, Ford drove the Unionists pell-mell back to their base at Brazos Santiago. Palmito Ranch was a lop-sided Confederate victory—Ford counted less than a dozen casualties—all wounded. Barrett's loss was severe—one of his regiments alone, the 34th Indiana Infantry, lost 220 of its 300 men. A few days after the engagement Rip learned of the collapse of the Confederacy the previous month but he had the satisfaction of knowing that he had maintained control of the Rio Grande for the Confederacy until the end.

Unfortunately for Rip Ford and for the South, he was never able to procure a Confederate commission during the war. His colonelcy was only a state commission and even the likes of General Magruder and other military and civilian leaders in high office could not convince Richmond to commission Ford in the Confederate Army. Although he drew the pay of a Confederate full colonel and was paid by the Confederate government while in command of the Rio Grande Expeditionary Force, he never wore the three stars and wreath of a Southern colonel. Ford's desire to stay in Texas, political intrigue, and jealousy of his superior officers kept the ex-Ranger from advancement during the war. Undoubtedly, Ford, with his military experience and great leadership ability would have risen to brigade or division command had he fought in the Army of Northern Virginia or the Army of Tennessee. When it came to combat leadership he was cut from the same pattern as John Bell Hood, Jeb Stuart and Patrick Cleburne.

Following the war, Ford, fearing prosecution by Federal authorities, fled with his family to Matamoros. He remained in Mexico but a few weeks, took his parole on July 18, 1865, and settled down in Brownsville. During the next ten years Colonel Ford would again dabble in Mexican affairs, return briefly to newspaper work and concern himself with politics. In the summer of 1866 he heeded the call of his old friend M. J. Carbajal who was aligned with the liberal Mexican forces of Benito Juarez. With some one hundred Texans, Ford crossed the Rio Grande to help Carbajal drive Maximilian's forces from Matamoros. Soon thereafter, Ford and his men were caught in a Mexican counter-revolution and discouraged by the strange quirks of Latin politics returned to American soil. With no further opportunity for military service, Rip once again turned to the newspaper business. He worked for a while as editorial assistant of the Brownsville *Ranchero*, then transferred his efforts to the Brownsville *Courier*. In the fall of 1868, Ford, in partnership with J. E. Dougherty, established the Brownsville *Sentinel*—a pro-Democratic paper. Along with his editing, Rip found time to occasionally guide cavalry patrols up the Rio Grande in an effort to curb the wave of cattle stealing from across the border.

By 1872 Ford was again flirting with politics. His editorials in the *Sentinel* had become so rabidly anti-Republican, that the Democrats of South Texas chose him as a delegate to the 1872 Democratic National Convention. The nomination of Horace Greeley, a Liberal Republican, as the Democratic nominee for president, so disgusted Old Rip that he swore off of politics temporarily and took the position as cattle and hide inspector of Cameron County. However, Ford, like a fire horse when he smelled smoke, couldn't resist becoming involved in a good political scrap, particularly when it happened in Texas and concerned the reconstruction government.

In the fall of 1873, the Texas Democrats nominated their first bona fide gubernatorial candidate since the war, Richard Coke of Waco. Opposed to Coke was the Radical Republican Governor, E. J. Davis, seeking a second term. A victory for Davis could and probably would have meant another two years of his hated police force and Federal occupation—conditions odious to ex-Confederates. Coke handily defeated Davis, but the latter refused to relinquish his office, claiming that the election was invalid due to a recent change in the Constitution. Austin was alive with excitement as both sides marshaled their forces for a showdown. Ford, foreseeing trouble at the capital, left Brownsville for Austin where the action was.

President Grant refused two requests from Davis to send Federal troops into the area, so the governor called upon a mixed white-Negro detachment of state police to keep the newly-elected officials from taking their seats. Coke in the meantime had asked for the support of a local militia company, the Travis Rifles, and had appointed William N. Hardeman, "Old Gotch" W. P. Hardeman, and Rip Ford as assistant sergeants-at-arms to guard the state capitol and grounds. The Travis Rifles, an all-white, well drilled and crack-shot aggregation had been organized and commanded by Ford in 1852. The unit had fought in the Civil War and had been reorganized after the war. During this crisis Ford again assumed command of the unit, marched it up to the capitol as the entire contingent sang the "Yellow Rose of Texas" and offered its services to Coke.

On January 16, 1874, newly-elected Governor Coke formally demanded that Davis and his cohorts evacuate the state capitol. Davis refused to budge and violence almost broke out at the state armory where Negro state policemen arrested the mayor of Austin when he tried to persuade them to surrender the building. The mayor was finally released but not until the Travis Rifles threatened to shoot a Negro state police captain. Tempers were running high and only a spark was needed to turn the city into a battleground.

On the following day Ford performed one of his greatest acts of public service for Texas and probably the South. Democrats, incensed by the cocky Negro troops and Davis' stubbornness, determined to physically oust the Davis faction. The armory, headquarters for Davis' Negro troops, became the focal point of the Democrats' ire. On January 17, a large armed mob gathered on Congress Avenue bent on assaulting the armory and killing the Negro garrison. The shouting, milling mass of irate Texans attracted Ford's attention as he left the capitol grounds. Hurrying to the scene of disturbance he arrived just as the mob was about ready to move on the armory. Old Rip, using the steps of a nearby home as a podium, chastised the crowd in his most picturesque language for its contemplated action and persuaded the leaders of the mob to desist from taking aggressive action. Ford warned his fellow Texans that if they carried out their threat of sacking the armory the state would be placed under a military government for many years. He then suggested that a company of volunteers from the throng be formed and march to the capitol grounds to assist the governor-elect in assuming his duties in a peaceful manner. Many members of the mob took Ford's suggestion and volunteered to march for the capitol, the rest melted away under Ford's stern gaze. Old Rip is one of the few men who could have controlled the excited mob. Many years later, W. P. Hardeman told Ford that stopping the mob from storming the armory in 1874 was the greatest contribution that Ford had made to his state. Hardeman ventured that had the mob carried out its aims "not less than 20,000 people would have been killed in two weeks—and Texas would not have recovered from it for fifty years—few even of those in the capital at the time realized the danger." Fortunately for Texas, Davis disbanded his forces, quit the capitol and vanished from the political scene.

During the autumn of his life, the versatile Texan continued his interest in public affairs and politics. He was elected mayor of Brownsville by a lop-sided majority in 1874; represented Cameron and contiguous counties as a delegate to the Constitutional Convention of 1875, and the following year was elected state senator from the Twenty-ninth District. As senator he championed for more efficient police forces and a better public school system. The last public office that the ex-Ranger held was superintendent of the Deaf and Dumb Institute in Austin from 1879 to 1883. Not content with merely supervising an asylum for illiterate handicaps, Ford introduced many educational innovations and curriculum changes that vastly improved the institute. Only the deterioration of Ford's health forced him to relinquish a position in which he had such a genuine interest—working with handicapped children and young adults.

In January, 1884, after recovering from his latest siege of malaria, the sixty-nine-year-old Ford moved to San Antonio with his family. In many ways the Alamo City was the center of Texas culture and letters and Ford conversed regularly with the many prominent Texans that had retired there. He spent the next thirteen years—the rest of his life in San Antonio—promoting and writing Texas history and was soon recognized as one of the outstanding historians in the state. Ford's journalistic skill and his participation in most of the outstanding events in Texas from 1836 to 1875 led him to write many historic articles for publication. He also contributed generously to the standard historical works prepared by James De Shields, Dudley G. Wooten, and Clement Evans. Ford, always interested in historical societies, joined the Alamo Association in 1894 and was one of the founding fathers of the Texas State Historical Association when it was organized in February, 1897. In fact, Ford wrote one of the first articles to appear in the *Quarterly* of the Association.

Rip Ford's most ambitious literary project was his attempt to write a history of Texas covering the period from 1836 to 1886. By the late summer of 1897 the "Memoirs of John S. Ford" as the short title of his history was called, had been written through the Civil War and reconstruction period. Unfortunately, he could not find a publisher but was sustained in his writing by generous friends and so continued with his work. In October, 1897 Ford laid down his pen and never picked it up again. He suffered a severe stroke and was in a coma for weeks. Finally on November 3, at the age of eighty-two, Ford died, and thus passed into history one of the most talented Texans of the nineteenth century.

In a brief ceremony, attended only by his family and a few close friends, Colonel Ford was laid to rest on the banks of the San Antonio River. An old Ranger, staring at the fresh grave was heard to say, "He rests by the bright waters of San Antonio in the bosom of his loved Texas, and 'after life's fitful fever' he sleeps well, the perfect ending of a good man."

Lawrence Sullivan Ross

Sul Ross, death of Peta Nacona -- December 18, 1860

Lawrence Sullivan Ross

by

Roger N. Conger

The name of Sul Ross is remembered in Texas for a remarkable variety of contributions and accomplishments. During his life span of sixty years he spent less than two of them as a Texas Ranger, and these at the very threshold of his maturity. In that brief period, however, were compressed action and renown beyond that experienced in most men's lifetimes. And during these same early years there were demonstrated those positive evidences of character which marked Sul Ross for future leadership, as a soldier and a statesman.

His years—the latter half of the last century—were those of rugged involvement for most men. When Sul's father, Shapley Prince Ross, arrived with his young family, Texas was still an independent Republic, a vast and sparsely-settled domain of river valley and prairie, rich and inviting to the home-seeker, but still menaced on the wide front by the unforgiving Mexican, and on another even wider by the embittered Indian. Two indispensable implements of every frontier family were the axe and rifle. Both of them were familiar and well used around the Ross household.

Leadership and love of action were inherent qualities for Sul. His great-grandfather, Lawrence Ross, of Virginia, had been wounded and taken captive by the Indians in about 1735, and kept for about ten years, until he was twenty-three years of age. Shapley Ross, Sul's father, was certainly one of the most colorful frontiersmen of early Texas history, and it would be entirely inconsistent to attempt a biography of the son without a preliminary brief review of some of the contributions of this remarkable sire.

Born in 1811 on the family plantation near Louisville, Kentucky, and losing his own father while yet just a boy, Shapley had struck out on his own at a very early age, even for those days. By the time of his marriage, when he was nineteen, he was already a successful and prospering dealer in horses and cattle, as well as an adept trader and intermediary with the Indians. They lived at several places in Missouri and Iowa, and in 1834, together with the families of several trusted friends, they settled at Bentonsport, Iowa, on the Des Moines River. It was the site of a reservation of the Sioux and Fox Indians, under the famed Chief Black Hawk, and the pioneers did well, although the severity of the winters began to tell on Shapley's health after a few years. It was into these adventurous surroundings that Sul was born, on September 27, 1839. His parents named him Lawrence Sullivan.

That same fall, his plans already matured, Shapley sold out his chattels at Bentonsport, loaded the remainder into sturdy wagons, with the best of his stock in the harness, and made the rugged overland trek to the great unknown of Texas. It was something of an ideal environment for men like this.

They chose to settle at the colony of Nashville, on the Brazos, where the oath of allegiance to the young Republic was administered by a truly kindred spirit, Neil McLennan. Like Ross, the Scotch McLennan had lived upon the farthest frontiers, and knew no fear.

Here at Nashville the Ross family opened up a farm, traded stock, and did the customary amount of Indian fighting. One close friend was Captain Daniel Monroe, who held title to a one-league tract of excellent land about thirty-five miles west, on Little River, where the city of Cameron now stands. After two years at Nashville, seven or eight families, including the Ross, joined Monroe in a move to this new location. It was choice land all right, but it was also much more exposed to raiding Indians, and it was here that Shapley first gained fame, and became a member of the newly-created Texas Rangers.

The first major incident was when a relatively small band of savages had come through the Monroe settlement by night and stolen every horse around. Early the next morning, as the settlers were fuming, a roving trader showed up, without any horses, but with several good-looking mules, which were immediately appropriated for the pursuit. The fleeing Indians, feeling that they were entirely safe, had not pushed their getaway, and the vengeful pursuers came up with them on Boggy Creek near present Georgetown, where all five of the raiders were quite shortly laid dead. Ross, and a nephew named Shapley Woolfolk, each had desperate, personal encounters with Indian warriors, and both emerged to recount the tales. The Indian dispatched by Ross, with his Bowie knife, turned out to be a notorious character called Big Foot, and Shapley at once became a hero along the settlements. He was one to his sons always.

Another significant episode occurred during these early years, when Sul was about four years old. Shapley had taken the boy with him one day to walk across to the house of a neighbor a mile or so distant, and the two were returning home when the father glimpsed a band of mounted Indians coming fast in their direction. Quick as a flash he threw the child across his shoulders, and bounded like a deer across the half-mile distance to home and the equalizing safety of his rifle. The Indians did not then press the attack, but Sul never forgot the experience to the day of his death.

Dangers there were aplenty; but it was the way of life, and the Ross household also knew much happiness and rustic pleasure. A charming incident took place in the early forties, on a day when Mrs. Ross was having a sizeable group of ladies in for a quilting party. After the big dinner at mid-day, the men were congregated at a nearby spring, supposedly engaged in enlightening talk, when somehow a keg of whiskey got into the picture. Some said it was brought along by a roving pedlar named Kattin Horn. In any case, it was too much whiskey at one time for such men, and most all of them were soon "grounded," but not before a good deal of rough play. Shapley fell or got pushed into the spring, soaking his leather breeches, and as he dozed a little later in the hot sun, these dried out as stiff as a board. A friend obligingly ripped out the seams so that he could get them off and stand up. Somehow word had got to the ladies that unusual things were going on down at the spring, but Mrs. Ross continued quilting placidly, and commented that there was really no reason for concern as she knew positively that Mr. Ross "never drank whiskey to excess." Just as she was saying this, Shapley appeared in sight clad only in a hunting shirt, carrying his leather breeches across his shoulder. It was said that the quilting party was "immediately adjourned."

Shapley rode and fought with the famed Jack Hays Company of Rangers, and participated prominently in an incredible catalog of adventures, against both Indian and Mexican enemies. It is more than likely that the youthful Sul rode with him, at least on scouting trips. We know that he did on one day in the early fifties, after the family had moved up to Waco. Raiding Indians had taken away a lot of good horses, including a favorite pony of the Ross', and when the pursuit party got together Sul begged so hard to go along that his father gave permission. The only available mount was a mule, and Sul rode it, accompanied thereon by a family slave named Armisted. However, when the settlers began to come up with the Indians it developed that the mule was absolutely terrified at their odor, became uncontrollable, and stampeded for the rear. Sul was furious at being thus prevented from having a personal part in the skirmish, which proved to be a minor one, but Shapley Ross later confided to friends his own pleasure at this early evidence of his son's spirit.

In 1845 Shapley decided, much to Mrs. Ross' gratification, to move into Austin, in order to provide the advantages of proper schooling for their growing family. He had recalled that when he had first announced their plan to emigrate to Texas, a relative had scoffed that the chlidren would have to grow up in ignorance. Shapley had solemnly vowed not to let this prediction come to pass. He had cleared 130 acres of good farm land there on Little River and owned another 160 acres of woods, all of which he traded to Captain Monroe for a wagon and yoke of oxen, just before the move.

It was at Austin, in 1849, that he was approached by Jacob De-Cordova, a leading land dealer and developer, and persuaded to make another move, this time up the Brazos to its confluence with the Bosque, at which historic crossroad DeCordova was just laying off the new town of Waco. Here Ross put down deep roots, being not only a founder but an involved and active citizen until his death in 1889. By that time he had lived to see little Sul elected Governor of Texas.

Much like his friend Sam Houston, Shapley Ross was patient and conciliatory in dealing with the Indian. But again like Houston, when friendly negotiations failed the purpose, he could hit, and hit hard. After 1850, with the heavy influx of settlers and the consequent expansion of the frontier, Indian difficulties became much more severe. The Comanches were particularly troublesome and aggressive, keeping both the Rangers and the United States Army on the jump. By 1855 the outcries from the frontier settlements had become so insistent the military decided to place all of the Indians on special "reservations," two of which were established. The one for the Comanches embraced four leagues of land on the Clear Fork of the Brazos River in Throckmorton and Shackelford counties. The other, of eight leagues, lay along the Brazos some ten miles below Fort Belknap in present Young County, and was intended to serve the twelve or thirteen tribes and sub-tribes of "sedentary" or agricultural Indians. Shapley Ross accepted an appointment to serve as Agent for the latter.

The hawkish Comanches neither knew nor cared anything about farming. And as for livestock raising, why bother when it was so much easier, and more profitable, to steal? Surplus animals were always in ready demand by the roving Comancheros, who by night drove them down into Northern Mexico. The reservation was doomed from the first to be a short-lived experiment.

One more of Shapley Ross' experiences, this while he was Agent for the "friendly" Indians, should be recorded. It was in early 1858, after an especially brutal Comanche raid which swept as far down as present Denton County. The settlers were up in arms, and Governor Hardin R.

Runnels called upon the Rangers for a reprisal. Captain John S. "Rip" Ford was encamped on the Clear Fork, directly between the two reservations, with a rather heavy force of 102 men. He at once held a conference with Agent Ross, who promptly recruited an additional force of just over 100 of the friendly Indians. Many of these were skilled scouts and trackers; and they all feared and hated the Comanches. On April 22 the force of 215 seasoned men trailed out toward the Comanche country, with an accompanying supply train which included two wagons, fifteen pack mules, and an ambulance. Shapley Ross was dressed in buckskins like his Indians.

Spring rains had carpeted the arid hillsides with grass and flowers. On April 29 the column forded the Red River and Ford began to dispatch small squads of scouts to push ahead. By the time they reached the mouth of the Washita there was much fresh Indian sign on every hand, and every precaution was taken to avoid giving an alarm. On May 10 the scouts killed a buffalo which was carrying two Comanche arrows, and the next afternoon they spied the grimed white cones of a Comanche village about three miles distant, on a prong of the Canadian River. Ford and Ross planned an attack for seven o'clock the following morning.

The first charge was fierce and decisive; but no one had ever overrun a Comanche camp without a battle, and this was no exception. Also, it soon developed that the village under attack was that of the widely-famed Chief Pohebits Quasho, or Iron Jacket, who boasted an ancient Spanish coat of mail which had "death so often dashed aside." Early in the battle the Chief appeared, wearing his famous armour, well mounted and surrounded by six or eight of his picked warriors, and led a fierce counter-charge upon a group of Ross' Tonkawas. But Iron Jacket's luck had run out, as the Tonks' first volley brought down his horse, and a moment later a heavy bullet pierced the ancient mail and drove it deep into the Chief's body. A second Chief quickly took command, only to be brought down a few moments later by a shot from Ross' Shawnee leader, Chul-le-qua. The battle became a rout and spread out over four or five miles. By mid-morning the Comanche survivors were in full flight, and the Rangers were rounding up prisoners and reckoning the list of casualties.

Ford estimated the number of Comanches engaged to have been about three hundred warriors. There were seventy-six found dead, plus eighteen prisoners, mostly women and children. The herd of captured horses, numbering over three hundred, was divided among the friendly Indians. The attackers lost only two killed and two wounded. But the entire force was physically played out and exhausted. On the return trip both supply wagons and the ambulance broke down and were abandoned.

The famous coat of mail was divided into several pieces, as trophies. Ross sent his to Governor Runnels, who placed it on display in the Capitol, where it remained until the fire of 1881 which destroyed building and contents.

Shapley Ross had some valued friends among the faculty at Baylor University, down the Brazos at old Independence, and in the fall of 1855 young Sul was enrolled there as a freshman student. The following year, however, for reasons best known to himself, the earnest, mature youngster rode horseback all the way from Waco to Florence, Alabama, to begin his second year there, at Wesleyan University. It was from this school he received his diploma in 1859.

In the summer of 1858, when Sul arrived home from school, one of the prime topics of local conversation was the Texas Ranger battle with Iron Jacket's Comanches. It was learned further that another such expedition into the buffalo range was already being shaped up, this time under the direction of the military. General David E. Twiggs at San Antonio had taken much interest in the recent Ranger victory, and had ordered the competent Colonel Earl Van Dorn at Fort Belknap to take four companies of the Second Cavalry and one of the Fifth Infantry and establish a supply base on Otter Creek, deep in Comanche territory. Van Dorn hopefully sent for Agent Shapley Ross, and inquired if it would be possible for him and his tested Indian allies to again go along. At this point destiny took a hand.

For one thing, Ross was feeling below par, physically. On top of this, his reservation Indians, although ready and anxious to go themselves, were highly outspoken in opposing the undertaking by Ross at this time. He was their father, so they said, and was more crucially needed for the duties and decisions at the reservation. One of the Indian leaders was Chief Placido of the Tonkawas, and it was he who finally appealed to Ross to delegate the expedition this time to the twenty-year-old Sul, who was quite probably taking an active behind-scenes part in the maneuvering. Van Dorn made no objection, after seeing how the Indians themselves felt about the matter, so it was soon settled. Sul Ross was to command the company of 135 Indians. Through Chief Placido they pledged him their unquestioning confidence and support.

It was early September before the impressive combined force moved westward out of Belknap. They forded Red River near the 99th meridian, taking again the same general direction as had the Ranger expedition, and established the supply depot on Otter Creek, at the edge of the Wichita Mountains, quite near the present eastern boundary of the Texas Panhandle. From here the scouting parties were fanned out daily.

Sul Ross sent two highly-trusted scouts, one a Waco and the other a Tehuacana, in the direction of a known village of the Wichitas, lying some seventy-five miles away, in present Rush County, Oklahoma. These two hit real pay dirt. As they arrived in the near vicinity of the village they found that a large band of Comanches, with about 120 lodges, under Chief Buffalo Hump, was encamped close by, trading and gambling with the Wichitas. Remaining well hidden until after nightfall, the two scouts slipped in and stole a couple of Comanche ponies, then beat a hot trail back to the base, to report their findings.

As Buffalo Hump's band had been the main objective of the expedition, Colonel Van Dorn could hardly bring himself to believe the news at first, and admitted later that he had even suspected some sort of trap. But Sul Ross soon allayed the doubt, and in short order the entire column was checked out and put in rapid motion, toward a very certain and very hot encounter.

Van Dorn's plan called for the well-tried early morning attack, and the tough and eager troopers clattered forward throughout the night. Including the time in battle they were in their saddles for an unbroken thirty-seven hours.

The action commenced with a wildly-yelling charge upon the horse herd, by Ross' Indians. The terrified animals stampeded in all directions, at one stroke putting most of the Comanches on foot. But it also steeled them to desperation, and they fought

> "Like adder darting from its coil,
> Like wolf that dashes through the toil—"

The terrain was difficult anyway, for the attacking cavalry, it being cut up badly with numerous ravines, into which the Comanches fled headlong, pouring back their return fire from the sheltering banks. They still were soon over-run, and fell back in disorder. Buffalo Hump made his own escape uninjured, early in the battle.

Sul Ross was in the midst of the action. With one of his Caddoes and two troopers he had cut off a group of fleeing Comanches, only to find them all to be women and children. As these were being herded together, several others ran by, one of whom Sul saw to be a white child about eight years old. He promptly ordered the Caddo to seize the child, a girl who fought like a wildcat. As this was taking place, the four were suddenly charged by some twenty-five Comanche warriors, and Sul looked clearly into "the bright face of danger." In an instant he saw the two troopers, Lieutenant Cornelius Van Camp and a Private Alexander, fall dead, the lieutenant with a Comanche arrow passing entirely through his body. Sul's rifle had misfired, and as he struggled to pull his pistol from its holster, one of the Comanches snatched up Van Camp's Springfield carbine and fired its heavy slug through Ross' body. As Sul fell he still tried to get off a pistol shot at his assailant, and recognized him as a truculent sub-chief named Mohee, whom Ross had seen at intervals around the reservation. The Comanche had already drawn his butcher knife, with the evident intention of removing the Ross scalp, when a sudden outcry from his hard-pressed kinsmen appeared to divert him and he started away at a run. Before he had made thirty feet, however, a well-directed carbine shot by another trooper brought Mohee to the ground. The Caddo scout was still holding onto the white child. It had been a very close call.

The attackers followed up vigorously for several hours, until the surviving Comanches had disappeared like blue quail among the sandhills. After the spoils had been removed from the lodges and divided among the scouting company, the entire village was effectually fired. The scattered horse herd was likewise rounded up and apportioned.

Van Dorn reported fifty-eight Comanches known dead, including two squaws. The victory this time was more expensive, too, to the invaders. In addition to Lieutenant Van Camp, the cavalry had lost a sergeant and three private soldiers killed. Van Dorn himself had a serious arrow wound, and Sul Ross' condition was critical. The heavy slug had somehow passed entirely through his body without striking a vital organ, but his suffering became so intense he begged at times for death to relieve him. He was given every comfort possible under the rugged circumstances, and was carried back along the return route in an improvised litter suspended between two gentle mules. His youthful constitution soon began to mend, and by December he was able to make the trip back to Alabama to complete his senior year at Wesleyan.

The white child, a little girl, who had been recovered so much against her will, had been brought back to Waco and given the best of loving care in the remarkable Ross household. Here she was soon gentled, and became a great pet. No trace was ever found of her original family, so Sul assumed the privilege of naming her Lizzie Ross, in honor of the Waco girl to whom he was paying serious court, Miss Lizzie Tinsley. The child grew up in the Ross family, and eventually married and moved to California, where her husband became a successful businessman.

Van Dorn commended Sul in the highest terms, in his official report, and while Sul was still recuperating at Waco a letter arrived from General Winfield Scott expressing his compliments and friendship. The way was assuredly open for a cavalry commission but the young veteran chose to pass the opportunity up and go back to college. In a letter written many years later Sul commented that he had received as his pay a dangerous gunshot wound, which was "still a painful reminder of the occasion."

These two punitive expeditions of 1858 did succeed in setting back the raiders for a while. With almost every hand against them, the several Comanche sub-tribes had been severely thinned and scattered. A year or more elapsed without further serious disturbance but the respite was too good to last for long.

By early winter, 1859, the marauders were again being reported from various points along the northwestern frontier. Then came another really brutal raid ranging across Parker County involving house burnings and several murders, in addition to the inevitable pillaging of livestock and other property. In early February the raiders were sufficiently bold to break into the mule corral at Camp Cooper itself and drive away the entire herd of sixty-three animals. The Governor ordered out a reconnaissance under the command of prominent ex-Ranger M. T. Johnson of Tarrant County, but it was poorly equipped and accomplished little. Information did come in that the Comanche sub-tribe called the Nokoni, or Wanderers, had been prominent participants in the latest outrages. Its Chief had taken the tribal name and was known as Peta Nocona. His vindictiveness against the white intruders was widely recognized.

Sul Ross had graduated at Wesleyan in June of 1859, and soon after arriving home at Waco he entered into informal but active service with one of the local companies of Mounted Volunteers. His record and reputation were evidently familiar to Sam Houston, for it was a very few days after Houston's inaugural in December that Sul Ross received a letter inviting him to the Capitol for a visit. He went at once, and the message was pointed. Houston offered him a commission as captain in the Texas Rangers, with orders to raise a company of sixty men from the Waco area, and with them operate in the general vicinity of Belknap. We may well assume that the offer came as no tremendous surprise to Sul Ross. He accepted it on the spot.

Returning to Waco, Sul experienced little difficulty in getting his company together. Almost everyone was acutely aware of the problem, and most of the men were ready and willing to lend a hand in correcting it. Before the end of that year, however, all of the Indians from both reservations were removed, with the assistance of Federal troops, to locations in the Territory, beyond Red River.

By spring, 1860, Ross' company was filled out, well equipped, and encamped in good comfortable Ranger style, on Main Brazos only a few miles below the fort. Scouting squads were trailed out regularly, crisscrossing a broad area to the west, on the alert for sign. It was scarce and scattered. An occasional rider, possibly hostile, was observed against a distant horizon, now and then, to be shortly swallowed up in the haze-hung sandhills. Around the Ranger camp there was always a bountiful array of fish and game—deer and turkey, antelope, quail and prairie chicken. Some of the finer marksmen took pride in picking off the heads of prairie chickens with their rifles, disdaining the scatter-gun.

Fall went by with no hostilities, and many of the men were becoming bored and restless. The Captain was positively relieved when word was brought in that an Indian camp of considerable size, and probably Comanche, had been sighted from long range, situated on the Texas side of Red River, and around two hundred miles westward from Belknap. It was decided in very short order to take the war into enemy terrain once again.

As Ross was required to leave a portion of his command at headquarters at all times, he selected forty to go, and easily persuaded Captain N. G. Evans at Camp Cooper to provide one of his sergeants and twenty troopers. He also sent word to the seasoned Captain Jack Cureton of Bosque County, who rode in shortly with seventy of his Mounted Volunteers. It was a "right, tight" little army that rode out towards Comanche country in early December, 1860. The supply train was of minimal proportions.

Winter weather had come early, with biting sleet and even snow, and the going was rough from the start. There was no grass, and many of the horses began to give out early. Before a single Indian had been seen, nearly half of the Rangers were traveling afoot.

About December 15 they reached one of the forks of Pease River, where the scanty timber provided some little shelter from the bitter "norther" that was blowing. As they moved along this stream they began to see sign. On the seventeenth large bunches of buffalo went past on the run. Sul knew they were getting close to target.

Ross and his Rangers were out early the following morning, and pushed ahead into the chill wind, that was also stirring up clouds of reddish, stinging dust. The cavalry was with them also. Cureton's civilian company was a little slower starting, but came on some three or four miles in the rear. The Rangers were moving quite slowly now, and were considerably concealed by the dust storm, when they suddenly cleared a slight elevation and found themselves looking at the Indian camp, no more than two hundred yards away.

The Comanches were busy breaking camp and loading pack horses, and were evidently entirely unaware of the attackers. But there was no time to wait for Cureton's men and the dismounted Rangers to come up. Without a moment's loss Ross ordered the cavalry sergeant and his twenty troopers at a hard gallop around some circling sandhills, to cut off retreat, and then, after a very few tense minutes' pause, the Rangers dashed headlong among the lodges with guns ablaze. The embattled Comanches boiled out like angry hornets, but as they fled rearward towards the sandhills they were met head-on by the cavalry. Ross described it in a letter years afterward, saying that "every Indian then fled his own way and was hotly pursued and hard pressed." Although it is likely that Sul did not know it at the moment, this was the village of Peta Nocona.

Seriously out-gunned, the Indians were very shortly over-run and fast cut down. In the surge of battle, Sul Ross caught sight of a large Indian spurring rapidly away, with a smaller one mounted behind, and a third following close on another horse. He quickly took out in pursuit, shouting to Ranger Lieutenant Tom Kelleheir, who accompanied him. It was a tight go, and the chase had gone a mile before the Rangers were close enough for a shot. Ross said later that he had hoped to get both of his at one shot, and his first fire did kill the rear rider, a girl, but the big man was wearing a war shield hanging down his back, which evidently deflected the bullet from Sul's Navy Colt.

As the dead girl fell, however, she dragged the man down with her. It was Peta Nocona.

The Chief was on his feet in another instant and sending arrows whistling at Ross, whose horse was plunging crazily with fear and excitement. Sul ducked as close to the saddle as he could glue himself, and fired as fast as he could manage any semblance of aiming. What the modest Captain described later as a "random shot" most fortunately did make connection with the Comanche's right arm, shattering the elbow and putting the deadly bow out of further action.

Ross slid to the ground with leveled pistol and called out to the Chief to surrender. In one letter in later years he said he shot Nocona twice more through the body. But instead of surrendering, the Chief stepped backwards against a small tree and began his death song, which Ross always described as having been most "wild and weird." Ross said that the Indian's desperate courage filled him momentarily with admiration and even pity. He was relieved when one of his Mexican scouts dashed up, carrying a lethal scattergun at the ready. As the two moved in closer, the Mexican called out again, in the Comanche tongue, but the Chief's response was a weak but savage thrust with his short iron-bladed lance. Sul nodded, and the shotgun roared.

Tom Kellehier had now ridden up with the third Indian a captive, but he was complaining profanely that it was only another dirty squaw. He had in fact been on the verge of shooting, when she had suddenly reined in her tiring mount and held up a small child she had been carrying under her blanket. But Sul took one keen glance and exclaimed that this captive was no Indian, but a white instead. She was bronzed by the sun and as dirty and unkempt as any savage, but her eyes were unmistakably blue. Comanches' eyes were black and glittery like a snake's.

The Mexican scout attempted a bit of conversation with the sullen creature, within his limited knowledge of her language, and did succeed in learning that she had been the dead Chief's wife, and that in the battle two of her older children, both boys, had managed to escape unhurt. It came to Ross at the time that she might just possibly be the very girl who had been carried away into captivity at the time of the massacre at Fort Parker, away back in 1836, but all efforts by himself and the Mexican failed to evoke, upon her part, any semblance of understanding or recognition.

Ross gathered together the dead Chief's weapons, which were later presented to Governor Houston. As the victors were rounding up such other spoil as the empty camp afforded, they stumbled upon another Comanche child, a boy of eight or nine, hiding like a jackrabbit in the wind-blown grass. He proved to be no relation to the Chief, and was terribly frightened until he became more reassured that his captors did not intend to kill him. Instead, he was taken back to civilization where he was reared and afforded a good education by the Ross family.

On the return trip, at the first night's encampment, the captive woman cried bitterly. Upon friendly questioning by the scout she gave him to understand that it was due not only to shock and grief at the death of Nocona but also from her fear and concern for the two young sons, Pecos and Quanah, now orphaned and cast upon their immature resources. They came through well, however, in later years. Quanah, the older, lived to become the principal Chief of his tribe and lived out his last years on peaceable terms with his white neighbors. The city of Quanah, in Hardeman County, was named for him in 1890.

Upon arrival at camp, Ross had the captive and her child taken over to Camp Cooper by the troopers, where she was afforded sympathetic attention by the soldiers' wives. He also sent a speedy communication to the home of Colonel Isaac Parker, who lived near Weatherford, in Parker County. Parker, who was an uncle of the lost girl, came immediately to Camp Cooper, and with the continued assistance of the interpreter, again took up the questioning. It was when Parker spoke the lost girl's given name that the first real light broke through. Staring as through a misty dream, the woman softly touched her breast and whispered—"Me Cynthy Ann."

She had lived as a Comanche for twenty-four years and seven months—too long for any easy transition. She did return to Weatherford with Isaac Parker, but despite the family's best-intentioned efforts it could never be home to the wild Comanche, and she tried repeatedly to steal away. The story spread, and she soon was the most famous Indian captive in the country, but her life was marked with tragedy. Just four years later, in 1864, Cynthia Ann died, at the home of one of her brothers in Anderson County. And the little daughter, called Prairie Flower, had already preceded her in death by several months.

After Ross had dispatched his report on the Pease River battle to Ranger headquarters, he forwarded a note to Governor Houston, along with the personal accoutrements of the dead Chief. A response was not long in coming, which read.

> "Your success in protecting the frontier gives me great satisfaction. I am satisfied that with the same opportunities you would rival if not excel the greatest exploits of McCulloch or Jack Hays. Continue to repel, pursue, and punish every body of Indians coming into the state, and the people will not withhold their praise."

But events of wider import were now stirring the state and community, and Sul had felt an overpowering impulse to take an active part in them. Houston was most keenly aware of them, too, but had taken his own unalterable position and fought vigorously to repress the irrepressible. In February Ross tendered his written resignation from the Rangers, with "regret and appreciation," only to have it returned by the Governor with another flattering letter urging reconsideration. But on the same day on which Houston had posted this communication, the citizens of Texas, by an overwhelming majority, voted the State out of the Union and, subsequently, into Civil War. Sam Houston went out too, and Edward Clark became the new Governor.

The Ross name was most familiar to Clark, and he too urged Sul to continue in Ranger service, especially in view of the extremely unsettled conditions then prevailing along most of the western frontier, which called for firm and diplomatic handling. Ross found it hard to decline the challenge and did pursue the assignment most effectively for Governor Clark for three or four more months. In May, he and Lizzie Tinsley were married, at Waco. A few weeks later his brother, Peter F. Ross, accepted a Captaincy in the Army of the Confederacy and began the recruitment of a cavalry company at Waco. At this juncture Sul dispatched his final report to Austin and volunteered as a Confederate private. His career in the Texas Rangers had come to a close.

The Ross record during the four years' war was matched by few if any other participants. Peter Ross' company was soon consolidated with the Sixth Texas Cavalry Regiment at Dallas. The first commander was Colonel B. Warren Stone, and Sul Ross was promoted to major. They marched to Arkansas, to be attached to the division of another sterling Texas Ranger, General Ben McCulloch, and were with him when he fell to a sniper's bullet at Pea Ridge in early 1862.

Dedicated to action, Sul experienced it aplenty from then on. Volumes have been written about his truly remarkable achievements in the military, and we will make a brief outline suffice here.

From the outset he was a highly popular commander with his fellow officers as well as with his men. In the fall of 1862, with a relatively high mortality rate among Confederate commanders, he was offered the stars of a brigadier, but, instead, requested and received permission to remain a colonel of his Sixth Texas. He was twenty-four years of age.

His ability and performance kept him constantly in the fore, and in October, 1863, during a skirmish at Yazoo City, Mississippi, he received a packet from Richmond which contained his commission as a brigadier general. As Victor M. Rose says in his *Ross' Texas Brigade*, "the appointment sought the man." At the war's end, Sul Ross had participated personally in 135 engagements with the enemy, and had come through without a serious wound.

He returned home to Waco a hero but an impoverished one. His family did own land, however, and there was more available at well-nigh give-away terms. So the warrior turned with his accustomed energy to the soil. Cotton, corn, and cattle paid a regular if moderate return. And everybody was in the same boat.

Events took an interesting turn in 1873, when a delegation of citizens paid a visit to urge Sul to become a candidate for the office of county sheriff. Once again there was considerable challenge. Many of the unpleasant sidelights of Reconstruction had been settled, but at Waco, directly across the shallow sandy bed of the Brazos, lay the vast and nearly untenanted Tomas De La Vega land grant. A sprawling sixty-thousand acre wilderness of scrub forest and creek bottoms, the tract had for years afforded secure harbor for desperadoes of all description—known among the more peaceable folks as "Modocs," after a particularly brutal tribe of Western Indians. Previous efforts to dislodge them or bring them to justice had been signally unsuccessful. Witnesses were so intimidated they declined to appear, and on several occasions some of the bolder bad-men had effectually taken over the Bridge Street saloon area and "shot-up the town."

Most likely Ross was feeling the need for some action anyway. He accepted the challenge and was promptly elected. His very reputation brought about an immediate reduction in the local crime rate, and to the more obstinate offenders he soon administered a liberal treatment of stern, unrelenting authority. By 1876, when young John Sleeper compiled the first city directory for Waco, he recorded in it that "the La Vega Grant has been purged of its law breakers. Good honest, producing citizens now inhabit and cultivate the land . . . over which the Modocs aforetime roved and committed depredations at will, with none to dare molest or make them afraid."

In 1875, when the Democrats of Texas had called for a Constitutional Convention to re-write the "radical" Constitution of 1869, the people of Waco elected the popular young sheriff to be their delegate. He applied himself with usual diligence and efficiency.

The keynote of the Convention was retrenchment and governmental economy, and the delegates carried this philosophy to the extent of declining to employ a stenographer to record the proceedings of their meeting. But the accomplishments of the body were highly popular and applauded throughout the State.

Sul Ross was by this time well established as a public-minded man who would get things done. In 1880, once again at the urging of many friends, he entered the race for the State Senate, was successful, and was re-elected in the campaign of 1882. He was serving as Senator when the State Capitol was destroyed by fire in November, 1881, taking with it, incidentally, the armor of Chief Iron Jacket, placed there by Sul's father so many years before. Sul saw the plans develop and materialize for the construction of the monumental new Capitol of red Texas granite, costing a bit above three million acres of West Texas land. And he became the first Governor to occupy the spectacular structure when he was elected Texas' Chief Executive in 1887.

He served as Governor for two progressive and productive terms.

At the end of the second term, in 1891, he was persuaded to accept the office of President of the Agricultural and Mechanical College at Bryan, a fine and growing institution which had been in existence for eight years, but had functioned up to that time without a formal president. His outstanding popularity brought rapid growth and expansion and assured its long-range objectives.

The death of Sul Ross was accidental, and in a sense as unusual as many of the experiences of his life. One of his chief recreations had always been in hunting and fishing, particularly in company with some congenial friends, and in the fall of 1897 he went with such a party on an outing for deer and turkey along the Navasota River, east of Bryan. A good comfortable camp was set up, and a Negro man went along to do the cooking.

They had learned beforehand that the location for their camp had always been highly popular with wood rats, so upon advice they carried along an ample package of rat poison, white and resembling flour. Their supply of flour for bread was in a wooden barrel. Just exactly when or how the rat poison got into the flour no one ever found out, but it did. One morning the cook prepared a batch of hot biscuits and within a few hours all of the hunters were more or less seriously ill. Sul Ross was deathly sick.

He was carried home with all the care and treatment possible, but he failed to respond, and died on January 3, 1898, just eight months before his sixtieth birthday. He was buried near his father Shapley, in the Ross plot in Oakwood Cemetery at Waco.

His love for A. & M. College and its goals is memorialized today by a fine bronze statue on the campus. And his broader interest in Texas education was recognized by the naming of Sul Ross State Teachers College at Alpine, in 1917. But to most residents, and to the devotees of the State's frontier history in particular, Sul Ross will ever be remembered and admired as the gallant young Captain of the Texas Rangers who fought and whipped the untamed Comanche, and brought the lost white girl, Cynthia Ann Parker, back to civilization.

Leander H. McNelly

Captain L. H. McNelly on patrol -- 1875

Leander H. McNelly

by

Joe B. Frantz

All classes of people play guessing games regarding the effect of certain death on their behavior. Although the sureness of death is known from what the Baptists call the age of accountability, no one really believes in such certainty and proceeds as if today and tomorrow will last forever. But then the doctor tells a man that he has six months to live— one month, one week, the remainder of this day; and for the first time a man realizes he is mortal and reacts accordingly. He takes that trip he always wanted to take, he writes a new will and gets his estate in shape for that other certainty—taxes, he makes a sentimental journey home, he re-establishes a proper relationship with his family, he whines and feels sorry for himself, or like the man bitten by the mad dog, he compiles a list of people he wants to bite before he goes.

Leander H. McNelly would have had courage if for no other reason than the fact that his parents had named him Leander. But he also knew he was going to die of tuberculosis at what the cliché-makers call an untimely age. And instead of drawing closer to his wife and children, or enjoying the 19th century equivalent of a protracted cocktail party, or grousing about the unkind hand which had been dealt him, he went to work various hundreds of miles from home, exposing his wracked body to hardship and to even quicker death, and faced the end of his life with a courage that made him seem oblivious to bullets and knives.

L. H. McNelly, as he preferred to be called, did not look or talk like a Texas Ranger, or even a Texan. He had come to Texas in 1860 from Virginia when he was sixteen years old, a small thin lad with a timid voice. He grew into that kind of man—small, thin, and timid. No one would have mistaken him for an emotional and career kinsman of Bigfoot Wallace, Jack Hays, or Bill MacDonald. Indeed, he was easy to ignore.

Unless, of course, you were trying to cleanse the earth of his presence. Then Captain McNelly acted like a Ranger, *was* a Texas Ranger. He had as much courage, as little patience with the subtle rights of the suspected or accused, as much racial arrogance, and as much intentness on enforcing six-gun law-and-order as any of the other notable and noticeable Rangers in that force's century of hyperactive history. He was capable of telling the United States Secretary of War—by telegram—to go to hell, and he did just that. And he made it stick. He is supposed to have originated the definition for courage—"you just can't lick a man who keeps on coming on"—a phrase now attributed to practically everyone who ever looked an enemy in the eye or shot him in the back. He would, again to employ the bromide, charge hell with a bucket of water, only in his case you could put money on his dousing the devil's fire. The only fight he ever lost was to an enemy that he couldn't see or touch—tuberculosis. Other than that, his career reads like all the Texas tall tales rolled into one, except that in his case they can all be proved.

For instance, a teen-age sheepherder turned soldier, McNelly had belonged to the Confederate Army since he was seventeen. Riding with General Tom Green's Mounted Volunteers as part of Sibley's Brigade, he had so distinguished himself at Val Verde in New Mexico that General Green made the youth, barely fuzzed over, his aide. At nineteen he became a captain of scouts.

McNelly's capture of Brashear City in Louisiana was portentous of the career ahead. With forty men under his command he ran into an estimated force of eight hundred Federals, plus two thousand blacks who had left the plantations to assist their liberators. A quarter of a mile from the Union troops was a long bridge which had to be spanned if the forty were to overcome the eight hundred. It was a task equal in improbability to that of an earlier young man's feeding the five thousand.

The captain hid his troops till dark. Then the entire forty began running back and forth across the bridge, shouting commands to unseen colonels and generals to move up on the right and left. For an hour they ran, noisily and heavily, before retiring. Forty men sounded like forty hundred.

At daybreak McNelly rode with a contingent of forty men—his entire crew—into the Federal camp, bearing a flag of truce and demanding unconditional surrender. Certain that the thousands of men on the bridge during the night were lying in wait, the Union officer happily accepted the terms; and Captain McNelly and forty men led the eight hundred prisoners to safety behind the Confederate lines, where General Green received them as happily as they had surrendered. They never did meet all the colonels and generals who had been on the bridge and on the left and right during the previous night.

Next McNelly, who had taken time off to take on responsibility for a wife and two children, showed up in 1870 as captain of a state police force designed by Republican Governor E. J. Davis to re-establish order and to assure the perpetuation of Republican control. According to Walter Prescott Webb, the state police came to stand for "official murder and legalized oppression." Allowing for Webb's Confederate and Democratic Party biases, the fact remains that the state police were hated by the substantial element of ex-Confederates who would soon rule Texas again. And that the outstanding former Confederate, Captain L. H. McNelly was leading a segment of the so-called "Texas Traitors." Why? *Quien sabe?* Perhaps at heart he was a man of action, and here was the group that promised action. Perhaps the routine of being a farming husband and provider had palled. Perhaps he believed sincerely in law and order, and without doubt Texas was turbulent. Again, who knows?

Certainly as a captain in the state police McNelly quickly became embroiled in the Walker County dispute which became one of Texas' major feuds. He was a victim there of a jailbreak, receiving a wound to match his Civil War injury from the battle of Mansfield. While convalescing, he told a Galveston *News* reporter of his distaste for Governor Davis and other law enforcement officials, none of whom were sufficiently forthright for him. Nonetheless he remained with the state police until it was disbanded in the spring of 1873.

When in 1873 Richard Coke and the Democratic Party regained control of the Texas political machinery, they inherited a problem of lawlessness and violence that makes today's turmoil look picnicky by comparison. In any direction from Austin, disrespect for authority—any authority except the rifle and revolver—prevailed. Walker County's feud was more of a symptom than a disease. From the outset Governor Coke faced the necessity of establishing some sort of restraining force.

Accordingly the governor re-established two military forces, the Frontier Battalion to reduce the Indian threat in West Texas and the Special Ranger Force to suppress banditry in the Nueces Strip between the Nueces River and the Mexican border. Whose banditry is debatable. Texans believed that all Nueces Strip sin originated with the Mexicans, whether from the north or the south bank of the Rio Grande. Reading the Mexican historian, Daniel Cosio Villegas for instance, one can hardly realize that he is reading about the same misunderstandings, for in the eyes of the Mexican nationals the *norteamericanos* were the *banditos*, forever violating Mexican territory, shooting peaceful Mexican herders and townspeople, and driving off Mexican cattle.

Take your choice. In a land with valuable property and almost total disrespect for ownership, life, and law the guilt has to lie on both sides of the racial and geographical frontier. Retaliation begs for and begets retaliation. If I shoot your *pariente* for his having shot my *pariente*, my action is not murder, only retribution, sanctionable by everything from the Bible through all the unwritten laws which mankind ever refused to write but chose to observe.

Add effective leadership in the guise of a charismatic man of dubious principles, Juan N. Cortinas, and you have a lawless condition that won't go away. Cortinas was respected or feared, or both, on either side of the Rio Bravo. He oversaw a loose organization dedicated to gathering cattle for shipments to Cuba and interior Mexico. He was a capitalist of stature, with foreign contracts. Also, he is either one of the Southwest's all-time unmitigated rascals and murderers, or he is an undersung hero still awaiting beatification into a true folk-hero. In his troubled land and times, nothing is certain. Either you could worship Cortinas for looking after the dispossessed and the Mexican-Indian, or you could denounce him as a relentless enemy of the Anglo, an inclusive term that embraced everyone except the Mexican-Indian.

What a leader he could have become among the Rio Grande Valley *huelgistas* of the 1960's! What a symbol he could have been for all the brown men at Resurrection City! What panic he could have shoved in the direction of the white establishment from Brownsville to Crystal City! Juan Cortinas, you were remarkable in your times, but *en verdad* you chose the wrong century.

Into this vortex of violence went spidery L. H. McNelly. But first, he began recruiting men from the Brazos country around Washington County. Average pay: $33 a month, plus food, ammunition, a rifle, and all the exposure and danger you could eat. Each applicant provided his own horse, saddle, and sidearm. According to N. A. Jennings, the Captain refused most Texan applicants, for fear that they might have to face the moral and emotional problem of shooting their own relatives. McNelly wanted men without doubts.

On his way to the Nueces Strip McNelly and his recruits stopped off in DeWitt County to deal with the "turbulent, treacherous and reckless" (his words) factions involved in another continuing, historic feud between the Taylors and the Suttons. Evidence in the Taylor-Sutton feud was not hard to come by; getting witnesses to court constituted the problem, not because the witnesses were timid but because they frequently died en route to the witness chair. When William Taylor was scheduled to be tried in early autumn of 1874 at Indianola, one hundred fifty Suttonites planned to attend "to see that Taylor got justice." Even McNelly decided that the cause of justice required reinforcements, which Governor Coke promptly dispatched. As McNelly reported, however, the tranquility was temporary, for both factions "have nothing to lose and everything to gain by a return to open warfare and will do all in their power to promote discord." Today's militants could take lessons.

But the Taylor-Sutton feud was only an interlude, a *divertissement* or *entr'acte* sandwiched into the main play, which was to be acted out in the Nueces Strip and give McNelly his lasting reputation. As the Captain delayed in DeWitt County, the anguished sheriff of Nueces County sent a telegram to Austin:

> IS CAPT MCNELLY COMING. WE ARE IN TROUBLE. FIVE RANCHES BURNED BY DISGUISED MEN NEAR LAPARRA LAST WEEK. ANSWER.

The answer, of course, was the arrival of McNelly in Corpus Christi, that most beautifully situated of all major Texas cities, unless you have a taste for mud flats and Houston. Corpus Christi, all sun and soft wind and pleasantry, was the focal point for Texas counter-raiding. Local armed citizens, naturally angry, were indiscriminate in their retaliations. If your eyes were black or your English were accented or non-existent, you must be Mexican and therefore a murdering *bandito*. Many a peaceful citizen of the United States, whose only sin was answering to the name of Sanchez or Navarro or Garcia, was gathered into the bosom of God before either he or His Maker was ready for the union. Even McNelly, neither a bleeding heart nor a racial liberal, was moved to protest:

> The acts committed by Americans are horrible to relate; many ranches have been plundered and burned, and the people murdered or driven away; one of these parties confessed to me in Corpus Christi as having killed eleven men on their last raid.

Probably McNelly is here guilty of imprecise English. More than likely, the killer boasted rather than "confessed."

To meet this extreme danger McNelly adopted an unusual defense. He passed over the latest model repeaters—Henrys, Spencers, and Winchesters—and chose for his troops the Sharp, a heavy, single-shot rifle in .50 caliber. It was a favorite among hunters of buffalo, which, it might be pointed out, seldom shot back. The Sharps had long-range accuracy, but were almost impossible to handle in a running fight. The McNelly philosophy showed through the choice; you don't waste ammunition spraying in a general direction—either you kill with your first shot, or forget it. As former Ranger George Durham told Clyde Wantland in the fascinating *Taming the Nueces Strip,*

> As time went on I came to know that right there was Captain's idea of fighting. He gave you one big chance; then you were on your on. You learned mighty quick not to bust that cap till you had your target lined up in your sights.

And so McNelly moved on down to the heart and soul—*corazon y alma*—of Cortinas' fief, Brownsville on the Rio Grande. Here he established a system of scouts and lookouts to report on outlaw movements. When on June 5, 1875, he received word that fifteen Mexican nationals had crossed the border below Brownsville, he set out to intercept. A week later he caught up with the raiders at Palo Alto near Laguna Madre.

The Mexicans headed home for the river, with the Rangers gaining. Bunching their cattle onto a small island surrounded by salt marsh, the Mexicans stood fast, apparently confident that their position could not be approached on horseback. They underestimated McNelly and his men.

Approaching the island from three sides, the Rangers charged directly across the salt marsh, holding fire till the last moment. The Mexicans could get off only a few panic shots, one of which killed a Ranger, and then broke. In the close pursuit the Rangers killed twelve raiders. Durham tells how one of the Mexicans left this world:

> Captain had his area quieted, except for one outlaw who was well hidden behind a clump of marsh grass. He wasn't firing any more, but he wasn't dead. Ten paces away, Captain called out loud, "My pistol's empty. Bring me some more shells." It worked. The outlaw broke cover, a knife flashing. He opened his mouth in a wide grin as he came charging. And Captain got him right in his big mouth.

In his official report McNelly did not mention having de-teethed the Mexican. Instead, he complimented his opponents: "I have never seen men fight with such desperation. Many of them after being shot from their horses and severely wounded three or four times, would rise on their elbows and fire at my men as they passed."

The practical result of the interception, presuming that death is not practical, was the recovery of 265 head of cattle belonging to the King Ranch, which in its turn could have been founded on land belonging to the Mexicans. The spiritual result, again presuming that death is not spiritual, was more telling. Cortinas had been served notice that the Rangers had arrived to put an end to banditry or recovery or whatever face you wanted to put on the activities. Thereafter Captain McNelly always spoke of having "naturalized" the invading immigrants! It was a naturalization process without recourse to reversal.

With their "no quarter" reputation rising, the Rangers experienced little difficulty for the next several months. Mostly the period from Palo Alto until autumn was spent in scouting and in improving the informer system, with only a stray individual action to punctuate the boredom.

But October terminated the comparative serenity. Through his spies McNelly learned that the Mexicans had a contract to deliver eighteen thousand head of cattle to Monterrey in ninety days. At a going price of $18 a head, a third of a million dollars was involved. For that volume of cattle and that kind of money, men like Cortinas could afford to risk the Rangers.

During the period from October 10 to October 25, the moon would be bright, ideal for moving herds. McNelly's men were tense with anticipation. But the period passed, and little happened.

But when a month later the moon rose bright and clear, Cortinas' men crossed over. McNelly received the news and the statistics, but that was all. About sixteen or seventeen Mexicans had entered Texas, and had left with about 75 head of stolen cattle. Although McNelly drove his men sixty miles in five hours, he was too late to intercept. At the crossing he found United States troops from the Texas town of Edinburg. They, too, had missed the raiders.

McNelly decided. For some weeks now he had been ruminating over a bold, illegal stroke designed to strike terror and restraint into the bandits' hearts. *He would ride into Mexico!* As early as November 12 he had written Adjutant General William Steele in Austin: "I should think myself in bad luck if I don't find some of their party on this or the *other side* of the river."

McNelly's move violated the territory of a friendly nation. From a legal standpoint he was clearly on untenable ground. So, he would have answered, Mexico is where the thieves are, and the thieves are what I am after. His action was illegal, immoral, indefensible. Also it was daring, dangerous, and unexpected by his quarry. Probably, like Laurence Sterne, I should here insert a blank page for the reader to insert his own ratiocinations on ethics *v.* effectiveness.

First McNelly tried to enlist the assistance of the Federal troops in his maneuver. Like a proper soldier the commander refused, promising, however, to "cover your return" if McNelly insisted on moving across. McNelly insisted. And persisted.

At one hour after midnight on November 19, 1875, Captain McNelly and thirty comrades pointed their way down the Texas side of the Rio Grande's sandy banks and splashed quietly toward Mexico. Somewhere "in there" lay the sleeping ranch of Las Cuevas, which doubled as a depot for stolen cattle. Ahead, also, probably slept a force of ten times as large as theirs. In his official report Captain McNelly tells the story succinctly:

> Before daylight on 19th I started for the ranch, found what I supposed was the Cuevas, charged it, found five or six men there, and they seemed to be on picket. We killed four of them and then proceeded on my way to Cuevas (a half-mile distant) and about three miles from the river; on getting within one hundred yards of the first house in the ranch, I found about two hundred and fifty or three hundred men drawn up in line. About one hundred mounted, the rest on foot, they occupied the ground and the corrals between me and the first house of the ranch. I at once saw the utter imposibility of taking a house by assault, as the firing at the other ranch had given them notice of our approach. After exchanging shots for about ten minutes, I fell back taking advantage of a few bushes on the side of the road to conceal my movements from the enemy.

McNelly beat his way back through the huisache and the cactus and the catclaw to the river, where he hesitated to swim toward safety for fear that a Mexican counterattack would catch his men in the middle of the stream. Instead, he formed them in a skirmish line, using the Mexican river bank as earthworks. Shortly the Mexicans, led by the owner of Las Cuevas, Juan Flores, arrived at the river. Seeing no Rangers, they thought the Texans had escaped to the opposite side and were almost at point-blank range when the Rangers opened fire. When the first volley took care of Flores, the leaderless Mexicans fell back into the brush.

On the United States side the Federal troops, not sure what was going on but certain that something was, abandoned caution and correctness, and some of them crossed to Mexico to assist. Not wishing to invite the entire United States Army, the Mexicans raised a truce flag, and promised to return the stolen cattle if McNelly would withdraw with his Rangers and take the Federal troops with him. On the next day McNelly, who earlier had refused a demand by the Secretary of War to get off foreign soil, received the stolen cattle on the Texas side of the Rio Grande. He had defied international law, in the dead of night he had invaded strange territory against an overwhelming force, and he had pulled off his raid without theatrics or heroics.

Did McNelly realize the untenable position in which he placed the United States? Possibly, says Webb, who believes that McNelly felt certain that if the exchange became intense, Federal troops would cross out of sheer excitement. Webb suggests that McNelly might have wanted to precipitate a war. Since McNelly never boasted and seldom disclosed more than the minimum, no one will likely ever know whether his invasion represented greater ambition than the mere recovery of stolen cattle and the punishment of a large band of Mexican miscreants. McNelly himself gives a bit of clue with his statement that he felt a surprise invasion represented his best hope—"dash into the ranch and take possession of the first house and hold it until the U.S. troops could come to my assistance—*and so told the officers before crossing.* I also told them that not one of us could get back alive without the aid of their troops."

If he didn't enlist enough Federal troops to justify a state of war, McNelly at least accomplished his first purpose. Tales of the daring Ranger raid spread throughout Texas and northern Mexico, with the result that the Ranger reputation for swift enforcement of justice was measurably enhanced to the point of mythology. No enforcement was surer than Ranger enforcement, it was felt in the States, while in Mexico the Rangers came to be hated to a degree that has barely abated today. To the Mexican on *his* side of the border, the Texas Ranger was the only animal more disliked than the Texan. To most Mexican-Americans today he is regarded as something less than an *amigo*.

From a practical standpoint McNelly's Las Cuevas War, as it came to be called, was successful. Border troubles diminished immediately. McNelly turned back to interior Texas to allay lawlessness among his own kind, including the notorious King Fisher. He even re-entered the Taylor-Sutton feud, which represented the same sort of assurance of a lifelong friend of little consequence—always there. Occasionally a fillip occurred, as when he varied the routine by arresting an accused murderer at his own wedding party. No record exists as to whether McNelly kissed the bride before taking her husband. Certainly whimsy was not part of McNelly's straightforward style.

In connection with the wedding arrest, five men stood trial in the court of Judge H. Clay Pleasants. Some question arose whether the trial might end in more shooting. According to Durham, McNelly intervened:

> Captain McNelly stepped from a door in the back and stopped at the end of the Judge's bench. He looked about the

same as he'd looked for several months, except he now carried in his right hand his service pistol, with the hammer back. He stood there till the talk stopped and things got quiet. Then he spoke in a voice that carried fairly well. "This court is now opening for regular business. Any man who lifts a hand to hamper its functions will die."

The man who quieted the court was only months away from dying of tuberculosis. Doc Holliday would have appreciated Captain McNelly. The performance was the more remarkable since by now McNelly was confined to his bed from weakness at least half of the time.

Three months later McNelly was no longer a Ranger, and McNelly's Rangers had been reorganized with Lieutenant Lee Hall in command. McNelly's name was officially dropped. The public notice said that the Captain had resigned for reasons of health, which in his case were certainly sufficient. But his friends believed that public and press criticism had forced his resignation. Adjutant General Steele explained somewhat unconvincingly that the Captain had resigned because of economy—his medical bills constituted one-third of the operational expense of the Ranger company. George Durham, who had joined his Rangers as a wee tad, probably tells the truer version: "All of us including Captain himself, knew he was down to be fired. His kind of law enforcing wasn't good politics." Even state legislators had made speeches against his alleged high-handed flaunting of procedures.

Allowing for the fact that Texas was still recovering from the legal abandonment of the Civil War and its aftermath, that the frontier portion of Texas possessed a justifiable reputation for violence, and that such notions as civil rights and criminal safeguards were minimal and regarded by most Texans with as much hostility as they display toward the Supreme Court nowadays, Captain McNelly still must be branded as brutal. He observed a code that few men—and he was one of the few—could live up to. He seemed impervious to pain, and equally oblivious of danger, except to his own men. He braved bulets with all the casualness of an apparition, and to a superstitious enemy was often believed to be incorporeal.

On a mission Captain McNelly rounded up all persons who might—*who might*—have some connection with the current trouble. He held them without warrant. If he suspected they were withholding information, he ordered them hoisted by the neck a few feet off the ground. Such an experience will induce many men to talk freely, even with sore throats.

In McNelly's company was Jesús Sandoval, a scout of Mexican-

American background. Sandoval's wife and daughter had been violated by Mexican raiders, and the retributive flame burned hot and forever in his passionate soul. If a suspect talked freely and coincidentally incriminated himself, McNelly turned him over to the pathological Mexican, who was inventive in his disposition of the presumed bandit and spies. Without condemnation Durham fills out the story:

> By the time we got there each bandit had been pulled loose from his head. Bound tight, each had been lashed to a tree by the neck; then Casoose (Sandoval) had looped the feet with his rawhide lariat and slapped his horse. That was it. Old Casoose had put his hat on the ground and was looking up, crossing himself. White foam was dropping off his chin and his eyes were blazing fire. . . . We didn't watch too long. My stomach was turning flips.

Qué éxtasi! Qué civilizado!

On the other hand, Webb would defend McNelly and Sandoval. So what, he asks, if McNelly permitted Sandoval "to send the spies to eternity by way of his paint horse gallows? McNelly did not have enough men to guard prisoners—he needed them all to fight. Nor could he have turned the spies loose without defeating the purpose for which he was on the border. . . . Affairs on the border cannot be judged by standards that hold elsewhere."

Larry McMurtry, who believes in absolutes rather than practicalities and delights in taking on anyone six months older than he and with an established reputation, criticizes Webb's admiration of McNelly as a "glaring whitewash." (*In a Narrow Grave*, Encino Press, 1968.) McMurtry, who can stand on his own without nitpicking at departed writers, tries to bring perspective to McNelly's actions in the following:

> Torture is torture, whether inflicted in Germany, Algiers, or along the Nueces Strip. The Rangers, of course, claimed that their end justified their means, but people who practice torture always claim that. Since the practical end, in this case, was the recovery of a few hundred cattle, one might dispute the claim. Only a generation or two earlier the Nueces Strip had been Mexico, and it is not inconceivable that some of the Mexicans involved had as good a right to the cattle as Captain Richard King or any other Texas cattleman. (Indeed, the Mexicans called them nañitas' cattle, grandma's cattle.)

In the current concern for proprieties McNelly's exploits can be lost sight of. With only two-score men, he cleaned up a situation. He displayed incredible courage, or foolhardiness, even for a man sure-marked for death. His last nine months were probably his most miserable. He retired to Burton in Washington County to farm, an old man barely into his thirties . He planned to raise cotton but never made a crop; apparently he lacked money to hire hands, and he was beyond working himself. On September 4, 1877—nine months after enforced retirement—he died, only thirty-three years old, almost half of them spent in some kind of violent service.

Was he one of those short-fused stars that burn out of time? Webb thinks so. According to him, McNelly should have been "at the Alamo or Goliad, or at some other place where his courage, ingenuity, and audacity could have been exercised in a patriotic cause. Had he performed the remarkable feats there on behalf of freedom that he performed in the Nueces Strip, mainly on behalf of a few stolen King cattle, he would have been a heroic figure. . . ."

So we leave the McNelly conflict to the moralists like McMurtry and to the admirers of audacity like Webb. Not to be invidious, but nonetheless like Alexander, like Jesus, like Mozart, like Schubert, like Gershwin, like William Walker—all the doers who died before forty—he flashed and disappeared. Only his was a constricted stage, and whether he carried within him the amplitude essential for greatness can never be known. He was the wrong man at the wrong time, although the men of McNelly's Rangers would never accept that verdict. Brutal or brace, he had made the most of the sorry body that God had outfitted him with. And in all things he was a man.

John B. Jones

Major John B. Jones and Sam Bass gang, Round Rock -- July 19, 1878

John B. Jones

by

BILLY MAC JONES

Late in the afternoon on July 19, 1878, Sam Bass rode into Round Rock, Texas, with two trusted companions, Frank Jackson and Seaborn Barnes. Twice previously they had entered the town to "look over" the Round Rock bank, and subsequently had determined to rob it on Saturday, July 20. But to take one last look, to be sure they had selected the best escape route, Bass had urged a third visit. This time as they rode toward the town, a less-trusted—indeed highly-suspicioned—fourth member of the gang, Jim Murphy, managed to leave the party at May's Store in Old Round Rock, allegedly to purchase a bushel of corn for their horses. Such was not his true reason, however, for a lethal rendezvous was in the offing, a rendezvous which, among the robbers, only Murphy could have anticipated. He had, in frontier parlance, "set it up."

Already present and secluded in a building near the bank were three Texas Rangers, placed there by their commander, Major John B. Jones, with instructions to "stay out of sight" until the road agents arrived. Jones had set his trap on the strength of a hastily-scrawled note Murphy had mailed to him two days earlier which read: "We are on our way to Round Rock to rob the bank. For God's sake be there to prevent it." With those betraying words, Murphy, an apparent accomplice of the robbers, had set Bass up. He did so through the persuasiveness of Jones, who promised the suspension of Murphy's impending jail sentence if he would assist the Rangers in bringing Bass to justice.

And justice was soon to be served, despite the fact that Jones and his three Rangers had arrived only the day before. Other Rangers were enroute to Round Rock but would arrive too late for the furious gunplay that erupted on that late July afternoon. The deployed lawmen hardly expected the action to begin when it did: Jones was half a block away in the telegraph office; Dick Ware, one of the Rangers, was awaiting his turn for a shave in a nearby barber shop; and the other two either failed to notice, or were not aroused by the casual way the bandits approached. Having left Murphy at May's Store, Bass, Jackson, and Barnes eased inconspicuously into the town, tied their horses to a hitching rail in an alley, and moved across the main street in the direction of Kopperel's general store next to the bank.

As the unidentified trio entered the store, Morris Murphy, a local law enforcement officer, thought he detected that one of them carried a concealed pistol. Deputy Sheriffs Grimes and Moore then followed the newcomers into the store. Grimes erred badly, for Major Jones had privately warned him that Bass might strike the town at any time. But almost as if he were oblivious to such a possibility, Grimes boldly inquired of Barnes if he had a gun. Then all fury broke loose. Barnes killed Grimes on the spot "for his inquisitiveness;" Moore fought back but fell to the floor with a gaping chest wound; and Bass was shot in the hand. The roar of gunfire brought the Rangers sprinting from their stations, and as the bandits ran for their horses, a murderous volley followed. Jones fired at them as he rushed from the telegraph office as did a few high-spirited citizens who also gave pursuit.

Seaborn Barnes never quite reached the horses; he was killed instantly by a bullet to the head. Bass collapsed from what would prove to be mortal wounds and had to be helped into his saddle by a gritty Jackson who managed to emerge unscathed. Then, holding a "pale and sickly" Bass on his horse, Jackson drove his own steed amid a fusillade of lead and miraculously managed to make good their temporary escape. By nightfall Bass knew he was dying and that it was foolhardy for Jackson to remain with him. A saddened Frank Jackson finally acceded to the pleas of his friend and quietly slipped into the darkness. Jones found the bleeding gunman alone the next morning, and despite prompt medical attention, Bass died the next day, July 21, 1878, ironically his twenty-seventh birthday. And in less than a year, Jim Murphy died a Judas' death—at his own hands. The Bass gang had found, as so many before them had, that John B. Jones always got his man. Actually, the Round Rock fight was the last major field effort which Major Jones directed as commander of the Frontier Battalion, an organization which called into new existence the Texas Rangers following a brief deactivation during the era of Civil War and Reconstruction.

Thus had two of the state's most skillful men of the 1870's met in mortal combat. Bass, the dashing nineteenth century Robin Hood who robbed and killed in a brief but spectacular four-year career as a highwayman, died amid the same violence by which he had lived. Yet his memory still lives in song and verse, and in a legend which insists that he was Texas' most beloved bandit. On the other hand Jones, despite his stellar performance in ridding Texas of some badmen, has all but slipped from historical perspective, as if cursed for having done his duty as a Texas Ranger. But those who knew the man knew also that it was his pride, not a lust for fame, which drove him relentlessly throughout the 100 days it took to track down Sam Bass and company, and which urged him to use all available means—including an informer—in order to fulfill his assigned duty.

Walter Prescott Webb correctly designated John B. Jones as the least known of the great Ranger officers, but he was also quick to reserve for Jones the pinnacle of praise: Of all the valiant figures in Ranger annals only Jones can be classified as a general. All of the rest, including Hays, Ford, McCulloch, and McNelly, were by comparison hardly more than rough-and-ready field captains. The evidence contained in the archival records on which Webb based his judgment is indisputable. To follow Jones' career in cleaning up the Texas frontier is a thrilling experience.

In spite of the fact that Jones frequently stood in the shadow of a victim's reputation, the Major was no lack-luster commander. He was "altogether one of the most dangerous men to criminals who ever lived." He kept his men constantly on patrol, ever alert, and ready for a fight. He drove himself and his men hard, always took the lead when raw courage was demanded, and never required of others what he was unwilling to do himself. Jones appeared to be more than satisfied with the respect and deference his men reserved for him, never thought of relaxing discipline in order to be popular, and never seemed to need his ego fed.

Governor Richard B. Coke commissioned John B. Jones to command the Frontier Battalion on May 2, 1874. The Battalion, sorely needed to bring a lawless, restive frontier under control, had been authorized only a few months before as a part of Texas' post-Reconstruction efforts to reestablish responsible government in all regions of the state. In the western regions, the task of establishing a respect for law and order appeared in 1874 to be almost insurmountable. Indians still roamed at will and plagued the frontier with their bestiality; badmen terrorized hapless citizens and robbed unprotected businesses; and feuds and racial tensions flared almost uncontrollably in areas where police officers were either virtually unknown or untrustworthy.

Worse, the frontier was almost without definite parameters, extending from Brownsville on the Rio Grande to Doan's Crossing on the Red River, and from El Paso in the west to the Panhandle in the north. To bring under control all of the lawless elements in so vast a region required a man with superior vision and comprehension. For the job, Coke chose Jones, "the littlest Ranger of them all," a man of slight stature, standing barely five feet eight inches tall, and weighing but one hundred thirty-five pounds! But Dick Coke knew his man—a man of "so much command and dignity in his manner" that no one ever "thought of him as small." The few men recorded as having made fun of him wound up either dead or in prison.

John B. Jones was born in South Carolina in 1834, moved with his family to Texas in 1838, and grew up on his father's ranch in Navarro County near Corsicana. He developed early a love for horses, became a superb horseman, and later raised his own blooded stock on another ranch near Frost. Contemporaries recorded that as an equestrian he had no equal: "He was simply irresistible on horseback." He received more formal education than most men of his day, even returning to his native South Carolina to attend Mount Zion College in Winnsboro. The Civil War gave him his first opportunity to demonstrate the quality of his training and the maturity of his judgment. He rose within a month from a private in Terry's Texas Rangers to the rank of captain and adjutant of the Fifteenth Texas Infantry. Governor Coke knew his record as a soldier quite well and felt no reluctance whatsoever in assigning him to the command post of the new Frontier Battalion.

Major Jones was as Spartan in personal habits as he was in field regimen. He shunned tobacco, loved buttermilk, and never, it is said, drank any drink stronger than black coffee. He dressed well, tastefully groomed himself, and rarely raised his voice either in social or professional conversations. And in the field with his companies, he lived exactly as they did, asking no special considerations and granting none.

His command consisted of six companies of seventy-five men each which he stationed at appropriate intervals north to south along the entire frontier. With a small escort, Jones rode from company to company, keeping them informed of developments and directing the total operations of the Battalion. The first assignment for the new commander, and the primary reason the Battalion was created, was the Indian menace. Frequent and almost paralyzing raids on unprotected settlements and ranches daily took their toll in people and livestock. Despite the presence of formidable U. S. Cavalry units along the frontier, small Kiowa and Comanche raiding parties moved about without significant opposition, at least until Jones and his men took the field against them. With the speed which was to characterize all of their efforts, Jones and the Battalion took less than a year to free the northwest frontier of Indian problems. Fifteen actions against the Redmen were fought, and numerous stolen livestock were returned to their owners.

Jones himself had a narrow escape in one encounter early in his tenure. In Jack County in the summer of 1874, he pursued into Lost Valley a band of Indians who had stolen some horses from a nearby ranch. From all signs, Jones estimated that not more than ten or twelve Indians comprised the raiding party and felt confident that his escort of twenty-eight men could handle the situation. Suddenly, his detachment rode headlong into a concealed band of Kiowas four times the Rangers' strength, a party led by the crafty Chief Lone Wolf and equipped with superior weapons. Escape was impossible, and the inexperienced troopers became somewhat panicky. But a cool Major Jones ordered his men to dismount and seek cover in a nearby ravine. Once steadied, Jones was able to rally them with a well-directed fire to meet repeated charges made by Lone Wolf and the Kiowas. Several braves were killed and Lone Wolf himself was unhorsed before the Indians withdrew to a safe distance. Frustrated by his failure, the Indian chief then ordered his warriors to kill the Rangers' horses with long-range buffalo guns, but not a Ranger was killed nor could the detachment be dislodged from its makeshift fortress despite a critical shortage of ammunition and water. One courageous Ranger was killed later in the day in a desperate dash to secure help, but no further success came to Lone Wolf. During the night, the Kiowas vanished, and Jones promptly marched his men back to camp, remounted them, and continued on his normal patrol.

By mid-1875, the Indians were subdued, but the work of the Battalion had hardly begun. All along the northwestern frontier, bands of desperadoes roamed unchecked, stealing and killing in complete defiance of local authorities. Jones and his men took up the cudgel and with amazing speed "thinned out the badmen." By December 1875, forty-five outlays were arrested and turned over to civil authorities; stolen property valued at almost $10,000 was recovered and returned to private owners; and at least two gunmen were killed. However, thinning them out was the best Jones could do, because a reported three thousand fugitives were at large on the Texas frontier.

Later in 1875, the Major was in Mason County where a conflict of major proportions was smoldering. Sometimes referred to as the "Hoo-doo" or Mason County War, the affair in reality was a feud involving German and Anglo residents. Some of the trouble resulted from old Civil War antagonisms; most of it, however, was the product of incessant cattle rustling. Residents of German extraction resented both the loss of their herds and the fact that it was almost impossible for them to obtain protection from the rustlers. Finally, when nine Anglo cattle thieves were arrested in February 1875, a semblance of satisfaction emerged—until four of them fled the jail before a trial could be held. Enraged by the escape, a mob took the other prisoners from the jail and hanged them. Anglos in Mason and adjoining counties swore revenge, and pledged to "burn the Dutch out of Mason County." The feud took a steady toll of lives until Governor Coke ordered Jones to the scene.

For four weeks Jones used persuasion, diplomacy, and force to quiet the rift. And in an effort to be impartial he even ordered away from Mason a company of Rangers known to be biased in favor of the Anglos. Another time he executed court orders for the arrest of John Clark, sheriff of Mason County, and nine Germans on charges he regarded as trivial but nonetheless substantive. In the end, peace came as much from exhaustion as from the Rangers' presence—but peace came without further bloodshed.

Off Jones went in early 1877 to Kimble County, another troubled stronghold of every sort of rascal, cutthroat, and thief. Men so openly defied the law that "forty to a hundred men could be raised in a few hours" to resist the conduct of any legal or court action. Cattle rustling and brand changing abounded, and owners dared not attempt to reclaim their pilfered livestock. Urgent pleas from residents brought Jones to the scene, and almost immediately the lawless breed showed their respect for the diminutive Ranger. Although they began "hiding out" Jones scoured every hollow, hill, and dale in the vicinity and eventually made forty-one arrests without bloodshed. And it is recorded that he took them to Kimbleville, chained them to trees, and protected Judge W. A. Blackburn while he held court under a live oak tree. Twenty-five of them subsequently were indicted for their crimes. And Jones again showed that he was tougher than the toughest in cleaning up Kimble County.

The once-violent and lawless frontier by 1877 was beginning to stabilize, thanks to some hard work by the Battalion and excellent leadership by Major Jones. Honest and law-abiding citizens were "much gratified" by the turn of events and became increasingly more dependable in helping the Rangers establish a respect for law and order. Still, two serious episodes in 1877—the Horrell-Higgins Feud and the El Paso Salt War—remained to be settled before a tired John B. Jones could leave the field, confident that his work was done and the frontier secure.

Major Jones never employed his great diplomatic skill to better success than he did during the Horrell-Higgins Feud in Lampasas County. A vicious quarrel developed sometime after 1874 between the two clans when the Horrells accused Pink Higgins of cattle theft. Subsequently Higgins turned the quarrel into a bloodbath by slaying Merritt Horrell on January 22, 1877, in a Lampasas saloon. Several members of both families were slain or wounded in running gun battles spanning the next six months. But into the melee stepped the ubiquitous Jones, who was determined to end the vendetta without further violence. Remarkably calm in his actions, he rode up to Mart Horrell's residence at sunrise on July 28 and arrested the entire Horrell party. And with but ten Rangers to aid him, he not only held his six prisoners without a jail but also took into custody three days later the three leading members of the Higgins faction. Even more remarkably, he persuaded the warring factions to sign a pair of unusual truce documents which asserted that "the past was forever buried with the dead." The results were almost incredible, for the truce held despite some later uneasy moments and the feud became "a by-gone thing."

Hardly had the ink dried on those documents before the Major was enroute again (October 4) to another trouble spot. In far-away El Paso, approximately four hundred miles from the nearest eastern settlement, controversy over the ownership of some natural salt deposits had stirred racial and international tensions to such a point that neither life nor property was safe from from assassins or mob actions. In earlier, more peaceful times, humble men from both sides of the Rio Grande had visited the salt flats near San Elizario and had eked out a marginal profit from their "mining" operations. A constitutional revision in 1866, however, removed minerals (including salt) from the public domain and assigned all mineral rights to the owners of the lands on which they were located, thus making unauthorized public mining unlawful on privately-owned lands.

Many of the lands were held by a very prominent claimant, Samuel Maverick, but some of the land rights remained perennially in dispute. An attempt to get the Texas Legislature to assign the remaining lands to public control failed for lack of local support, and a bitter political battle involving public and religious officials resulted. Finally in 1877 Charles Howard, an El Paso district judge, filed a successful claim to the disputed salt lands and announced that trespassers on the flats would be prosecuted. Incensed Mexican peons rioted, took Howard into custody, and forced him under duress to surrender his claims. The mob also demanded that he leave El Paso forever.

He left, but only for four days, and returned to gun down Don Louis Cardis, another local dignitary whom he blamed for his reverses. Again riots broke out and civil authority in El Paso County became non-existent. It was at this point that Governor Richard Hubbard ordered John B. Jones to go immediately to El Paso and take charge of the situation. Since none of the Frontier Battalion could be moved rapidly enough,

Jones went alone (one riot, one Ranger), but if he felt any apprehension about the matter he did not betray it with his actions. He studied the scene closely, saw how serious it had become, but believed he could control the mob at least for a few days. With his usual intelligence, he tactfully advised the rioters that he had come not to settle the salt question but to keep the peace. The legal question of salt rights was properly one for the courts to decide. Then, after some deliberation, he secured a pledge from the disgruntled crowd that they would "keep the peace," and he won their confidence by persuading Howard to surrender for trial. Relative tranquility was restored, and the Major soon decided that his presence was no longer needed. He sent for a detachment from Company C, Frontier Battalion and placed John B. Tays, an El Pasoan, in command. On November 22, Jones departed for Austin, fully satisfied that the situation was stable and that the Rangers were capably commanded.

But Jones erred in his judgment; Tays did not possess the qualities of a good Ranger. He lacked initiative and the ability to think clearly in a crisis. And he promptly lost control. Charles Howard, out of jail on bond, surprisingly obtained a new injunction against further unauthorized use of the lands, and with a small Ranger force (later enlarged by Tays and twelve other Rangers) Howard set out for San Elizario to enforce the court order. Even though Howard technically was in the right, the mob responded again with a show of force, surrounded Howard and the Rangers in the San Elizario Ranger Station, and ultimately forced Tays to surrender Howard to a firing squad. Howard's crude death, and the subsequent mutilization of his body, stunned the entire county, and a precarious peace ensued. Local authorities were able to regain control, but Tays was forever discredited and embarrassed.

Saddened by the misjudgment of Tays, Major Jones returned to El Paso to serve as Texas' representative on a board of inquiry sent to investigate the entire episode. His efforts on the board were not marked by enthusiasm. The final report, which he approved with minor reservations, was filed on March 16, 1878, just four months before his encounter with Bass—the last action he personally directed for the Frontier Battalion.

Jones had proved himself to be a great field commander, to whom diplomacy always was preferable to bloodshed. He always sought to handle all men fairly and to make arrests without having to resort to violence. Only once during all of the field actions he personally directed did he fail to accomplish these ends—the shoot-out with Bass at Round Rock—a remarkable feat in view of the unbelievable boldness of the frontier desperadoes with whom he dealt. Significantly, Major Jones retired from the field shortly after Bass was killed, and he then assumed in 1879 the post of Adjutant General. Isolated pockets of Indians and thieves still existed, but Jones entrusted the last jobs of taming the frontier to younger men such as George W. Baylor at El Paso, C. L. Nevill at Fort Davis, and G. W. Arrington in the Panhandle. He continued to direct the activities of the Frontier Battalion from his desk in Austin until his death on July 19, 1881.

His tenure as commander of the Battalion lasted less than five years (May 1874 to January 1879), and when he left the field the Frontier Battalion already was an anachronism. The once-great menace of frontier lawlessness and anarchy was all but broken completely. Jones' name may not often be mentioned in the legends and popular accounts of the Texas Rangers, but the lawless breed in his times knew him well and feared him. His contribution to the stability of the state was both dramatic and unique; by taming the frontier with his special group of Texas Rangers, he speeded the state's development and returned the Rangers to the very heights of service and efficiency.

He may have been little in size and short on fame, but John B. Jones stands tall in deeds.

★ ★ ★ This book is printed on Warren Olde Style paper. Text type is 10-point Regal. Chapter headings and half titles are handset in 18-point Americana. Composition by Fred Jones, page design by Billy Don Shirley. Printed by Davis Bros. Publishing Co., Waco, Texas. Color plates by Advertising and Marketing Associates, Waco, Texas. Color consultant, Travis Lawson. Book layout by Bob Davis, Texian Press. Binding design by Frank J. Jasek, Library Binding Co., Waco, Texas. Half-title drawings, title page drawing and original paintings by David Sanders, Austin, Texas. This first edition printed September, 1969.